I

"Ben Swenson brin[illegible]
fascinating stories b[illegible]
pearing history. From forgotten gold mines and the site of John Wilkes Booth's fiery demise to the haunting hulls of wartime concrete ships, Swenson's debut book is grounded in primary source research and sheds new light on America's past and her fading relics."

—Christian Di Spigna, author of *Founding Martyr: The Life and Death of Dr. Joseph Warren, the American Revolution's Lost Hero*

"Much has been written about the well-preserved sites where America's history occurred, but this intriguing book by Ben Swenson takes a different twist. Some of the nation's most storied places have been lost to time—disintegrated, buried, or surrendered to the forces of nature. Swenson takes readers on an engrossing journey to find the East Coast's lost history and explores the lessons that lay in the wake of decay."

—Dr. Bruce M. Venter,
president of America's History LLC

Orphaned Heritage

Orphaned Heritage

The East Coast's Disappearing History

Ben Swenson

ISBN (Paperback): 978-1-962416-90-0
ISBN (eBook): 978-1-962416-91-7
Library of Congress Control Number: 2025905574

Designed by Sami Langston
Project managed by Andrew Holt

Printed in the United States of America

Published by
Brandylane Publishers, Inc.
5 S. 1st Street
Richmond, Virginia 23219

brandylanepublishers.com

For Adah,
A well of grace and inspiration.

Contents

Introduction

On the Trail of Disappearing History

It's hard to say exactly how the *William T. Parker* managed to drift along the Atlantic coast all the way from North Carolina to Maine and back again without a soul on board, only that such a remarkable feat makes its present condition a sad postscript.

The *Parker* was small for a three-masted schooner, just 105 feet long. Built in 1891, its deep hold and wide main deck were perfect for hauling lumber from coastal forests to builders in New York and Massachusetts. Crewmen recall wood stacked nine feet high on deck.[1]

A century after its glory days, the *Parker* isn't recognizable anymore. All that's left above water is one pitifully decayed gunwale, the rotten, spongy wood studded with rusted iron pegs. The hull sits in an out-of-the-way cove, a watery pauper's grave, with a dozen or more forgotten old ships all in different states of ruin.

But once upon a time, the *Parker* was a thing of beauty. Wilson Jackson, one of numerous North Carolinians who served on the crew of the *Parker* in 1907, recalled the ship's beauty in Cecil S. Bragg's *Ocracoke Island: Pearl of the Outer Banks.* Those old schooners were "trim and proud in full dress; their white sails gleaming when struck by the rays of the sun; a shapely copper-tinted forefoot stepping daintily from sea to sea like a young girl dancing."[2] Jackson and other seamen loved the boat, which became affectionately known as "The Old Parker" and "The Flying Dutchman of Baltimore" in Chesapeake Bay ports of call.[3]

As idyllic a portrait as Jackson paints of the *Parker*, the working life of a sailing ship was rarely so pure—they were at the mercy of seas that were nasty as often as they were nice. The *Parker* was no stranger to calamity; it ran aground frequently and capsized at least five times, spilling its deck load into the sea. Every time, the *Parker* owed its salvation to capable captains, the United States Life-Saving Service, and inexplicable luck.[4]

"Her stern hit hard on the bottom," Jackson recalled of one such grounding off Ocracoke Island during a ferocious storm. "The blow shook her from keelson to truck. Her bow was in the wind and her sails were slatting and popping like small cannons . . . she fought for inches at a time from the sucking ocean bottom. She canted over as the sails finally filled and off she went to deeper water."[5]

Years later, during another harrowing ordeal off the Carolina coast, the crew abandoned ship and left the *Parker* for dead. That's when the old vessel scoffed at that betrayal and cruised the entire length of the East Coast and back unmanned, as if to show how misguided that vote of no confidence had been. After being recaptured and serving for another twenty years, the *Parker*'s career as a workboat truly ended in 1935 when it collided with a steamer off Bloody Point, Maryland. The damage was so crippling that repairs weren't a practical option, and the owners forced the *Parker* into retirement after a forty-four-year run.[6]

Today, the *Parker*'s wild adventures and pet names are history. The chance that the boat would live on in popular memory, much less in physical being, was tiny. There was never a connection to war or glory, never any reason to keep the *Parker* around. I found what's left of the ship one bright morning in Stansbury Cove, a bulge on the industrial shoreline of Baltimore's Curtis Creek. Beneath the static of traffic on Interstate 695, a grassy knoll overlooks the *Parker* and the adjacent skeletons. At the foot of a gentle slope is a boat ramp just feet from the derelict hulls.

You need not look hard to find abandoned history. This is the fate of nearly all that has passed. When memory fades, what's left succumbs to decay. The fortunate conditions of preservation and interpretation are exceptions to the rule.

Whether that loss is well-known or not, it is always lamentable. Within each of these lost causes lies insight—about the past and the future, about ourselves and each other. Look hard enough, and there's wisdom in those fading whispers. And that's to say nothing of the value in acknowledging people who took part in these dramatic episodes. Remembering is a tip of the hat to their courage and sacrifice, the fate that placed them in a remarkable time and place.

In the chapters that follow, we will embark on a journey to find the East Coast's disappearing history. This is not an adventure in urban exploration, also known as urbex, which involves a fascination with abandoned public, industrial, and domestic buildings. Urbexers brave all sorts of mortal dangers, not to mention fines and arrests for trespassing, to stand among ghostly ruins that often appear stuck in time. No, all the sites included in this book are not only publicly accessible but also relatively easy to get to.

We'll be exploring history that could have been preserved, and probably should have been in a perfect world, but for a variety of reasons, wasn't. Some of these stories are well-known. Others few people will recognize. Nature wasted little time reclaiming the material remains and, in some cases, threatens to absorb any surviving fragments. Part of the narrative is the wild world that's taking over the places where human dramas once unfolded. But nothing can ever erase what happened, and we'll discover, in each location, the lessons that float in their wake.

Those derelict ships like the *Parker* decaying by the shores of the East Coast's cities tell of countless shallow coves well past redemption, cluttered with industrial debris, hindering what might be more helpful habitat. Perhaps that means that it would be better for them only to exist in memory, with a few simple physical keepsakes securely stored, protected for future generations. At the Chesapeake Bay Maritime Museum in St. Michaels, Maryland, Chief Curator Pete Lesher showed me a stanchion that had been removed from the *Parker*, a small but enduring testament to its life. Maybe that's how the *Parker* should best be remembered.

On our voyage together, we will visit a land that remains scarred to this day by our lust for wealth. We will travel to a place where the ground beneath our feet has been on fire for more than a century. In a river gorge, we will find that a return to nature has included some unwanted invaders. We will talk to people who hope to preserve disappearing history, not only for its cultural value but for its potential to bring revenue to rural communities. And we will visit a forgotten highway median where soldiers captured and killed a presidential assassin. But our odyssey begins long before popular memory, in the footprints of this land's ancient human inhabitants, discovering what they left and the water that threatens to erase those faint traces forever.

Chapter 1

Shell Middens: The Drowning Traces of Ancient Footprints

Long before Europeans colonized the New World, American Indians shaped the land. The indigenous inhabitants had two of the elements they needed to move mountains: time and manpower. By about fifteen thousand years ago, they had fanned out across the Americas—from the frozen tundra of the Arctic to the tip of South America. There's no exact figure, but good guesses pin the peak population of Indigenous Americans as high as 112 million.[7]

Long before European contact, American Indians were prolific builders, constructing towering pyramids, intricate mounds, and irrigation systems. But not all feats of engineering were as flashy or as deliberate. In many cases, though, they were just as permanent, and exist today on shores that humans have inhabited for millennia.

History has recorded in fine detail the dynamics of the centuries after contact—treaties and wars, promises made and broken—a compelling saga that won't be any more robust with a cursory retelling here. Suffice it to say, countless American communities suffered the same fate as that of the Timucua, a group of some three dozen chiefdoms in what is now northern Florida and southern Georgia, who were defined by their shared language rather than by political or cultural unification. When Spaniards set foot in the Timucuan home range in the mid-sixteenth century, the culture numbered more than fifty thousand. Within a century and a half, that population had plummeted by 95 percent thanks to disease and warfare. A century later, the Timucua were extinct.[8] Even so, the landscape continues to tell the stories of the Timucua and of countless other tribes who can no longer tell those stories themselves.

The notion that Europeans arrived on the American continents to find unspoiled wilderness shortchanges Native Americans' effort and ambition. Indians were eager landscapers and likely had a hand in notable large animal extinctions. Among their favorite tools was fire, which could help regenerate terrain that was both arable and enticing to game, which they hunted prolifically. They likewise removed trees they couldn't use and planted groves of nut-bearing species that aided their survival, manipulating local ecosystems to their advantage.[9]

And like consumers today, they left trash, most of which simply vanished over time. But for tribes that resided where tidewater offered a bountiful buffet, there was one consumer staple that wouldn't go so quietly.

"He was a bold man that first ate an oyster," wrote seventeenth- and eighteenth-century author and satirist Jonathan Swift. Bold or not, that imaginary pioneer certainly had some packaging to toss. And he probably did that not too far from the spot where he slurped the slippery and nutritious innards. The shell had staying power because of its composition of calcium carbonate. It was the start of something monumental.

Middens are trash heaps—layer upon layer of shells discarded in the same place by succeeding generations of coastal diners. They exist wherever there's a body of water with an edible shellfish population at hand, on each of the six inhabited continents, from the banks of freshwater rivers in Australia to the saltwater coasts of Ireland. The East Coast of the United States abounds with them, too, from Florida to Maine, thanks to countless inlets and estuaries teeming with edible bivalves.

American Indians relied on this ready pantry. A single shell—indeed, an entire meal's inedible remnants—can hardly change topography. But, through untold generations of repetition, the mundane task of eating oysters can generate memorials to the civilizations they outlast.

I met Keith Ashley at just such a historic monument at Timucuan Ecological and Historic Preserve in Jacksonville, Florida. Ashley is a professor of anthropology at the University of North Florida and an expert on shell middens. He was kind enough to lead me on a guided hike one muggy Florida afternoon through six hundred acres of protected woods at the Theodore Roosevelt Area of the Timucuan Preserve, named in honor of the nation's great conservationist.

Ashley and I hiked under the dense canopy of a Florida forest: an understory thick with palmettos and Spanish moss cascading from the hardwoods above and swaying in a soft, tepid breeze. We passed the incongruously well-maintained grave of the Browne family, whose patriarch, eccentric loner Willie Browne, offered the grounds of his sprawling hermitage for indefinite preservation.

There was no threshold marking our arrival, but about fifteen minutes into our hike, the shells began to peek through the earth. We had come to a massive midden made by ancient Timucua. The scale was hard to imagine. A mature wilderness carpeted the midden's crown, concealing the scope beneath a dense mat of vegetation. This midden is huge: some twenty-five acres and, in spots, twenty-five feet deep. Two shells—a single oyster—were mere grains of sand on so large a landform. There were too many to count in layers beneath our feet, as far as we could see.

The terrain at the preserve is rolling, covered in an old forest with leaf litter and a dense understory. The midden undulates, and there are high spots and low spots in no particular configuration. At places where a small slope is near vertical, gravity has pulled away the blanket of leaves and offered a peek at what's beneath our feet.

I asked Ashley about how much time it took to create so large a landform, but he deferred. "You have to know the size of the workforce," he said. "And in the case of the people who made this, we're not sure."

He didn't commit, either, to a construction timeline. "We're not sure if this was a seasonal camp or if they came here for three years, wiped out all the shellfish, moved on, then came back when the population had replenished itself."

Nevertheless, the midden tells of a land that sustained Timucua people for generations. "The Timucua people were fisher folks and shellfish collectors," Ashley said. "They came to farming relatively late—no earlier than about 1450. The bounty of the estuary met all their needs."

But middens provide us with more than broad strokes. Like a

modern trash can that offers detectives usable intelligence, this midden offers details where a written record is silent.

Middens preserve themselves. The shells remain largely intact, even when a thriving forest grows above them. The calcium carbonate has the added advantage of safeguarding all the other stuff inside the midden, too, because it creates an alkaline container that inhibits decay of things like pottery and bones that would normally break down.[10]

Preserved shards of pottery have helped Ashley estimate the ages and timelines of specific middens. Anthropologists have a firm understanding of the time periods when American Indians used different materials to temper their pottery or make impressions in it. When they observe these qualities in excavated pottery, they can identify the timeframe in which that pottery and its surroundings were discarded. Some of the oldest middens are accurately dated to 3000 BC, about the same time the potter's wheel made its debut in Mesopotamia.

Likewise, bones preserved in middens yield insight into contemporary ecology as well as the diets of the people who left those bones behind. Many of the bones come from the small fish that one might expect in the diets of such prolific shellfish eaters; these provide a glimpse into the historical aquatic ecosystem. But even among the skeletal remains of local fishes and terrestrial animals that American Indians ate, there are some surprises. "We've found two passenger pigeons," Ashley said, referring to a species that once comprised a quarter of all birds in North America but were hunted to extinction around the turn of the twentieth century.[11]

These middens represent a vast swath of time. Twenty years is how long historians estimate it took laborers to construct the Great Wall of China and the Great Pyramid of Giza. And while individual middens might be smaller in scale, their creation took much longer. "Some of them have a span of two millennia," Ashley said.

Naturally, once a midden grew large enough, it was a feature that Indians lived on rather than beside. Indeed, some middens might have been terraced or have taken the form of a pyramid. With his trained eye, Ashley discerns features in the underbrush that anyone else might not notice—the barest trace of a half-moon ridge of shells, for instance, likely the grave of a Native dignitary. It's common, Ashley said, to find the preserved remains of Indians among the shell, whether it's during archaeological excavations or construction. The middens are not only historical, they're also sacred: testament to a vanished and vanquished people, a time machine that has frozen historical moments in a three-dimensional matrix. They're a reminder that in ourselves and all our everyday comings and goings—procuring, feasting, dying—lies the deliberate action of many millions of predecessors. And that adds some sting each time a shell falls from the midden into obscurity.

Middens disappear for several reasons. Ashley and I ventured down a dozen or so feet of slope to the water's edge, where a marsh covers the broad basin of the St. Johns River. Far in the distance, a crane loomed over a small patch of industrial shoreline. Outcroppings revealed a bank of shell that would soon fall into the water. Erosion is common, Ashley told me. Lots of middens once sat adjacent to marshes like this, but over time, parts of them have washed away. Some have been covered with dredge spoils taken from the channels of North Florida's heavily trafficked thoroughfares. But there is another manmade threat that accounts for much of the middens' losses.

Ashley and I stopped at a place where the gentle slope of the midden's surface abruptly gave way to a sharp disturbance, a bowl-shaped depression perhaps fifteen feet across. This was the void of a miner's haul.

Oyster shell has been a valued commodity in the past several hundred years because of its wide range of uses. Settlers along the southern Atlantic coast mined middens, burned the shell to make lime, and added other basic ingredients such as sand and water to create a concrete called tabby. Today at Kingsley Plantation in Jacksonville stand the remains of twenty-five cabins that once housed enslaved laborers. While most of the cabins are missing their roofs, the tabby walls are still standing strong two hundred years after their construction.[12]

Miners carted off shell in vast quantities to line footpaths and roadbeds and to level less-than-horizontal lots. Parts of this particular midden became agricultural fertilizer and mortar for bricks. Shell was versatile and cheap, which is why people took large chunks out of middens well into the twentieth century. "What you see is only a percentage of what was once here," Ashley said, gazing over the marshy basin of the St. Johns River.

Ashley would love to do more detailed study of the midden we visited, to core it and see how far down it extends in different locations before reaching sand. While the National Park Service oversees thousands of archaeological investigations on its properties around the globe, there are no plans for such work here. This historical site sits on high ground, meaning that the forces that destroy middens, such as erosion and sea level rise, are not as immediate as they are elsewhere. There are countless other threatened sites that would benefit from prompt attention because their struggle for existence is urgent.

It's unreasonable to expect that every midden everywhere will be permanently preserved, Ashley said. There are far too many of them. Early American Indians found value in seaside settlement like modern Americans do. But legislation could be improved, he said. Right now, middens on private property can be more or less altered or destroyed at the landowner's whim, without a moment's pause for reflection on their significance. Such destruction threatens not only thousands of other middens in Florida, but also many others along the entire span of the East Coast.

Eleven hundred miles from Jacksonville as the crow flies, the Damariscotta River is a quintessential Maine waterway, a short tidal nub that ebbs and flows daily with brisk tidewater from the Atlantic Ocean. Two thousand years ago, the Damariscotta was home to an oyster population of such profound longevity and abundance that ancestors of the Etchemin people built the largest shell midden north of what is now South Carolina.[13]

For more than a millennium, Native populations feasted there on innumerable shellfish and other sea animals until, scientists surmise, changes in the salinity caused the oyster population to plummet. More than a thousand years of oyster roasts left behind a sloping mound, nearly four hundred feet long by 125 feet wide—think of the dimensions of an American football field, including the end zones—and at least fifteen feet deep, but in places perhaps double that. The contour resembled a whale's back, and the name stuck: Whaleback Shell Midden.[14]

What Native populations had taken a millennium to create, though, entrepreneurs efficiently removed in a blink. From 1886 to 1891, the Damariscotta Shell and Fertilizer Company mined the vast majority of the midden's contents, over two hundred tons of shell, which it ground up for a poultry feed additive.[15]

Yet even in the late nineteenth century, when eagerness for "progress" trumped developing notions of preservation, there were people who realized what the world stood to lose. A professor at Harvard's Peabody Museum paid one Abram Gamage two dollars for each ten-hour day spent standing by the excavation and removing the archaeological treasures that plunked out. Among the artifacts that Gamage sent back were pottery and stone tools, antler tines (presumably for opening the oyster shells), and charcoal. And, of course, bones—fish and fowl, deer, dogs and, yes, humans.[16]

Today, what was once the Whaleback Midden is a state historic site co-managed by the Coastal Rivers Conservation Trust. An easy trail that begins in a sloping meadow leads hikers to the erstwhile mound. Maine's agreeable summer climate makes for a quick and pleasant stroll through the remains of this vanished history, which nature has covered with a lush forest. Yet traces of Whaleback's former stature come through in the abrupt and unnatural changes in topography and in the oyster shells that peek through the ground cover, remnants that avoided excavation.

Modern hikers on that trail can gaze across the briskly flowing waters of the crystal, blue-green Damariscotta and see a similar—though smaller—midden. The tall, bleached wall outcropping on the sandy shore was named the Glidden Midden after the owner who defended the mound from eager miners. Today, the University of Maine upholds Glidden's legacy by sponsoring citizen-scientists known as Maine Midden Minders, whose mission is to monitor and document the status of as many of the state's roughly two thousand remaining shell mounds as they can.[17]

Most middens are not as grand as the behemoths in Florida and Maine. Most are low-slung affairs that are shallow and broad, barely elevated above the water that, sooner rather than later, will be their ruin. It's happening right now.

I visited just such a place with a descendant of the people who made one of them. Daniel Firehawk Abbott is a member of the Nause-Waiwash Band of Indians who descend from the Nanticoke people of Maryland's Eastern Shore. Dorchester County sits on the eastern edge of a portion of the Chesapeake Bay and has more than fifteen hundred miles of shoreline. Scientists have identified some thirty middens in Dorchester, but there are likely more in this county and thousands in the bay at large.[18]

Abbott and I struck out in kayaks one foggy morning to see one of them. Much of Dorchester County is marshland, and swift-moving, ribbon-like creeks turn randomly through vast expanses of whispering reeds. In Dorchester's marshes, Abbott hears the breath of his ancestors. "Their spirits still wander these lands," he said.

But Abbott, or any observer, need not perceive this land's ancient inhabitants through a sixth sense. Dotted throughout the spongy terrain of the marsh, their trash remains. The first midden Abbott led us to was a hummock among endless expanses of marsh near the end of a widening bay. A swift ebb tide took us there. Here this midden, perched at the rim of a retreating marsh, showed itself in cross section, a vertical, foot-and-a-half face of oyster shells right at the waterline.

"This was their cool-weather camp," Abbott said. "The biting insects are unbearable here in the marsh during the warm months. They would have been inland during that time."

And while this midden is narrow compared to similar ones elsewhere, it is just as telling. Abbott fingered through the shells that had fallen from the midden into the shallow water at the edge of the creek and found pottery, stone tools, and large rocks that are unnaturally cracked—evidence, he said, that the Natives were using them to heat water.

Abbott's visit today is as much a gesture of acknowledgment and remembrance, a visit he makes occasionally as a sort of requiem for those who were here before him. Because soon enough, low-lying middens like these will be washed over, permanently buried at sea.

Part of the problem is that land in many stretches of the southern United States is slowly sinking because of a phenomenon called subsidence. One reason is geological. Glaciers blanketed much of the northern half of North America during the last ice age, and when they melted, the bedrock beneath them began lifting away from the Earth's core, liberated from the weight of all that ice. Like half of a seesaw, the continent's southern half began moving downward.[19]

But groundwater withdrawal, especially in the region of the lower Chesapeake Bay, is the chief cause of subsidence. People take vast quantities of water out of aquifers for industrial and personal use, which causes layers of clay to compact. Industrial operations use an especially high amount of water. In a couple places where there are large factories, subsidence is nearly triple that of the region at large.[20]

Rising seas, too, threaten to inundate middens. Sea level rise is well documented. Ice caps at the Earth's poles are melting, adding to the volume of water that fills the oceans. Global ocean temperatures are also increasing, and water expands as it warms. What's more, the changing climate disrupts ocean currents, which means that in places like the Chesapeake Bay, less water is drawn away from shorelines on an outgoing tide.[21]

What that means for the long, low stretches on tidewater's fringes—the very spots where nearly all the middens exist—is that they'll undoubtedly be inundated by even a modest rise in sea level. Scientists estimate that, here in Maryland, a 1.4-foot rise in the mean sea level is reasonable by 2050. Fifty years beyond that, a fair estimate adds an additional 2.3 feet. In that scenario, the vast majority of Dorchester's middens, those exactly like the one here, will be under water.[22]

Abbott and I waited for the tide to turn, alone with these silent messengers of the past. I looked over the broad marshes to the gray water of the western horizon, the water that would slowly inch above the ground beneath our feet. When the flowing tide had built up enough thrust, we nosed our kayaks into the current and let the water guide us inland, to the boat ramp, to higher ground—worlds away, centuries away from these ancient flats.

Seas have been rising for thousands of years, and there's no telling how many middens have already slipped beneath the waves. Still, some historians and scientists are trying to stem the tide to give future generations the possibility of dry middens to work with and to acknowledge the historical and cultural worth of these sites. Little can be done to stop the sinking land and rising seas, but there are ways to put up a fight against what's hastening their disappearance.

Cape Canaveral is an apostrophe on Florida's otherwise gently sloping Atlantic coast. The landform is perhaps best known outside the region as the home of NASA's John F. Kennedy Space Center. Twenty percent of the infrastructure that NASA has constructed anywhere exists on the sprawling sixty-six-square-mile complex, including a couple launchpads where spacecraft from the Apollo and Space Shuttle programs blasted off. The problem is that all this sits a mere five to ten feet above sea level at best, a precarious position to be in with seas rising so fast.[23]

In 2012, Hurricane Sandy passed two hundred miles off the Florida coast on its path to a direct hit farther north, yet the wave energy that battered Cape Canaveral pushed oceanside dunes landward sixty-five feet. Although that was a remarkable event, it was neither unprecedented nor isolated. Hurricanes will always be a part of life in this region of the world.[24]

What most people don't realize about Cape Canaveral is that it's also the site of perhaps hundreds of middens. The largest and most famous of them, Turtle Mound, is a midden so tall that sailors once used it as a navigational aid. Turtle Mound sits inland, protected in Canaveral National Seashore. But many middens at Cape Canaveral don't have the same sort of insurance.

Professor Linda Walters showed me just such a place. Walters is a professor of biology at the University of Central Florida and an expert on intertidal zones, that piece of land and sea that's sometimes covered with water and sometimes not. That small sliver is key for preservation; the life that thrives there has the potential to safeguard the dry land behind it. The intertidal zone is a rich biological community that functions as a thriving ecosystem comprised of members with especially useful traits. Or that's how it's supposed to work, anyway, according to Walters.

At the midden where Walters and I met, many hundreds of years had compacted the layers of shells into a sturdy substrate. At the shoreline of a narrow bay called Mosquito Lagoon, the sheer face of the midden drops abruptly to the water below. Some of the erosion has come from the powerful energy of storms like Hurricane Sandy, but human intervention shoulders an equal share, especially in inlets.

Walters gestured out over the wide, brown water of Mosquito Lagoon. "Sometimes as much as sixty or seventy boats will pass through here an hour," she said, and it's their wake that gives the shoreline a constant pounding.

Traditional methods of stabilization wouldn't work here. Something like a seawall or riprap breakwater would be too costly. And they're out of line, anyway, with the gentle touch that's often preferred on national lands. But most of all, they don't work. A hard surface simply deflects wave energy back into the body of water, and that energy bounces around until it finds a surface that absorbs it, which often happens to be land opposite or adjacent to the seawall.[25]

What Walters has found instead is that a living shoreline can absorb much of the energy and protect the upland surface behind it, too. Along this stretch of midden, Walters and assistants had laid artificially created mats of oyster shells and planted marsh grass and red mangrove. The idea was that that shell would recruit new oysters, and the flora would take root and spread naturally through rhizomes under the surface. Life, given a little encouragement, would thrive.

This and other stretches of living shoreline Walters helped create have taken off. The marsh grass and mangrove are, indeed, spreading, providing suitable habitat for other shoreline-stabilizing species. Walters looked to a mangrove seedling with all the tenderness of a loving gardener. It's a volunteer, she said.

At water's edge, the intertidal zone, rich with color and texture, teemed with life. A blue crab darted away at our approach. Seaweed swayed with the slowly pulsing waves. "There are 149 macro species that inhabit an intertidal zone like this," Walters said, and named just a handful—sponges, seaweed, shrimp, fish small and large. It's also growing shoreline. A 2013 study by one of Walters's graduate students showed that a living shoreline like this can add nearly five vertical centimeters of sediment to the shoreline.

Important for the eroding midden behind it, however, is that the living shoreline is absorbing the energy in moving water, no matter how it's caused. All those shoots and shells take the hit, and the midden doesn't have to. The exposed shell is no longer the water's punching bag. "This living shoreline may not look like a lot, but it is," Walters said.

The beauty in this approach, she said, is that it's easy. Schoolchildren can make the oyster mats and grow marsh grass and mangroves for replanting in kiddie pools. Ten thousand or more already have. Walters was once monitoring a site when a young boy and his father happened upon the shoreline. *Look*, the boy told his father, *I helped make that.* "The only way this works is if the community gets involved and is invested in this," Walters said.

Ultimately, community conversations and action will cement middens' fate, and that won't come without a reckoning. We need to ask ourselves what will be saved and what will be surrendered, because resources and efforts are not limitless. Walters is introspective. "How much do you save? How much do you preserve for future generations? How much do you let go?"

The Indians who created these middens were simply living, and certainly gave little thought to the trash that would outlive them. They couldn't have imagined that the end of their lineage would come from the wide ocean to the east, that the same expanse that washed in tidewater, that washed in life, would also usher in the end of the world as they knew it. The least we can do is protect some portion of these monuments to their memory.

Chapter 2

Gold Lust: Glittering Dreams that Scarred the Land

The easy money is gone. The scars are there to prove it. But for those willing to stake a claim, there's still a fortune to be made in gold.

Gold is as valuable today as it was to the legendary kings and pharaohs who adorned themselves with it. While it is true that it remains a symbol of high status—British monarchs still arrive to their coronations in a four-ton gilded carriage—it is also as close to a universal currency as it's possible to get. Pulling this shiny rock out of the ground is the closest one can get to harvesting a money tree, so throughout history, at the first murmur of easy gold, ambitious dreamers flock in droves.

Although gold is found on all six inhabited continents, it's an indelible part of the American story. Decades before prospectors moved west in 1849 in the California gold rush, however, the East Coast encountered its own frenzy: an extraordinary story of lucky strikes and unimaginable wealth, raucous boomtowns that went bust as quickly as they sprung up. But most of all, gold made mountains of disappointment. Some two centuries later, there's a landscape near the Eastern Seaboard profoundly changed by the rush for riches. Although most of the recoverable gold is long gone, crafty entrepreneurs still seek fortunes in its glittering legacy.

Though the Cherokee or their ancestors had long known of the presence of gold in the Appalachians, the southern Appalachian gold rush didn't begin until 1799 when a farm boy from western North Carolina found a seventeen-pound gold nugget that would be worth well into six figures today. The family used it for a doorstop until they discovered what it was. His father sold it for $3.50, about $260 today.[26] For nearly three decades, the hardy homesteaders and backwoodsmen who peopled that remote stretch of the Tarheel State combed through rivers for other such lucky strikes, and as it turns out they found them, including another massive nugget that weighed twenty-eight pounds.[27]

By the time gold was found in Georgia in the late 1820s, the manual on gold rushes had already been written. When prospectors flooded into hilly North Georgia, the landscape was doomed to be damaged so deeply that it would take centuries to recover.

Mystery shrouds the discovery of gold in North Georgia. Here's the scene: Lumpkin County, Georgia, 1827. Or 1828. Or 1829. Or not even Lumpkin County at all; the story changed a few times. The most widely accepted version is that Benjamin Parks—Uncle Benny Parks to some—found a giant gold nugget on his birthday. But it might have been his slave. Or someone else entirely. No less than five other competitors have claimed they found Georgia's gold first.[28]

Panning for gold is, perhaps, the method most commonly associated with the metal's extraction, but it was hardly the most widely used or most effective. Gold lies in thin veins that snake through the quartz beneath certain areas of North America: what's now the western United States, Alaska, and the Yukon, as well as a thin belt under the eastern foothills of the Appalachian Mountains stretching from North Georgia to Washington, DC. The sinewy veins of gold are not uniform in diameter or depth, the result of random and violent geologic forces billions of years ago.[29]

Riverbeds in these gold-bearing regions were once peppered with gold that had eroded from bedrock, most often as tiny flecks that tumbled downstream, to be buried by bigger rocks. On relatively rare occasions gold plunked into the water as certifiable nuggets that sat among river rocks, waiting to make men rich.

Naturally, the riverbeds were the first places that prospectors looked. There in streams, knee-deep in rushing water, early prospectors panned, swirling scoopfuls of water and sediment into the shallow metal disks, deftly ditching worthless rock and sand until all that remained were sparkling specks. Panning's relative accessibility and low cost made it one way to look for Georgia's gold, but it was slow and could only process pay dirt one small panful at a time. Serious miners always kept a pan on hand, but used heavier equipment to go faster, a method called placer mining.[30]

Devices designed to wash gold-bearing gravel encountered a rapid evolution during Georgia's gold rush, but the successive designs had features in common. A long, narrow box with an open top sloped downward at a low angle. Prospectors dumped sand and gravel from a gold-bearing riverbed into the higher end of the flume, then washed it through the contraption with river water. There to catch the heavier components, which included the gold, were parallel riffle bars—speed bumps, more or less, just high enough above the base of the box to snag the desired rock. Miners would often line the riffle bars with mercury, which attracted gold like a magnet. Using variations of these implements—devices with names like "rocker box" and "long tom"—miners scooped out the riverbeds of North Georgia many times over.[31] But the amount of gold accessible on river bottoms paled in comparison to what remained behind in the hillsides, embedded in quartz.

Miners who wanted to extract the gold-embedded quartz, or gold ore, had to dig horizontal tunnels, or adits, and vertical shafts to get at the richest veins. In Georgia, these shafts could be more than a hundred feet deep, though the average depth was just a quarter of that. Miners first hoisted or wheelbarrowed ore out of these mines. The next step for the rock was a stamp mill with one or more pistons, often powered by a waterwheel, that crushed the ore to the consistency of sand. Operators could then pan out the gold or divert the ore over mercury-covered plates to collect the valuable rock.[32]

These destructive methods marred the landscape quickly. In 1848, a correspondent from Washington, DC's *Weekly National Intelligencer* wrote a dispatch from his visit to the heart of gold country, Dahlonega, Georgia. "On approaching Dahlonega," he wrote, "I noticed that the water courses had all been mutilated with the spade and pickaxe, and that their waters were of a deep yellow; and having explored the country since then, I find that such is the condition of all the streams within a circuit of many miles. Large brooks (and even an occasional river) have been turned into a new channel, and thereby deprived of their original beauty. And of all the hills in the vicinity of Dahlonega which I have visited, I have not yet seen one which is not actually riddled with shafts and tunnels."[33]

But where the natural landscape was destroyed, local economies boomed. The town of Auraria, Georgia, symbolized the free-for-all population explosion that lit up North Georgia during the gold rush. In 1832, Auraria was a one-horse town known as Nuckollsville, named after the owner of the tavern and hotel at the town's heart. The earliest residents lived in a handful of no-frills cabins. But that changed after Georgia officials began the 1832 Land Lottery.

State lawmakers had been giving away tracts of land to qualifying citizens by means of lottery since 1805. The final land lottery took on special urgency when it became apparent that much of the land to be given away contained gold. Lottery officials began conducting drawings for forty-acre parcels in the heart of gold country in October 1832. Overnight, Nuckollsville transformed from a sleepy waystation to a boomtown. "There is in this village 20 or 25 stores, 18 or 20 lawyers, 4 or 5 taverns, a printing office, Doctors, Barbers, Billiard Tables, & C—and in all making about 1000 inhabitants," wrote William L. Gwynn in January 1833.[34] As a sort of homage to the town's sudden vigor, residents shed the name Nuckollsville in favor of a more appropriate moniker: "Auraria," derived from the Latin word for gold, *aurum*.[35]

Benjamin Parks himself, claimant to the title of Georgia's gold discoverer, noted the influx of hopeful prospectors. "They came afoot, on horseback, and in wagons, acting more like crazy men than anything else. All the way from where Dahlonega now stands to Nuckollsville there were men panning out of the branches and making holes in the ground."[36]

Ultimately there were three thousand people in Auraria and upward of twenty thousand in the gold fields of Georgia, North Carolina, and South Carolina altogether. Ethnic differences, chronic food shortages, insufficient housing, and dim prospects—only a minute fraction were statistically likely to walk away with riches—made daily life in the gold fields a precarious existence.[37]

"Brother James lives here in the heart of the gold region in the village of Auraria—in a log cabbin [*sic*] that I can scarcely stand upright in," wrote Gwyn. As for his brother's neighbors, Gwyn had an even gloomier assessment. "I have never before been amongst such a complete sett of lawless beings. I do really believe, that for a man to be thought honest here, would be a disadvantage to him, or at least he would be set down for a fool and treated accordingly."[38]

And in Auraria, Dahlonega, and the rest of gold country, a number of establishments sprung up to allow miners to indulge their vices. Saloons were common, as were brothels and venues for gambling and other games of chance. But miners' camps were also a popular place where the gold rushers "gathered around light wood fires, at night, and played on the ground and their hats, at cards, dice, push pin, and other games of chance, for their day's findings," according to one eyewitness. With so many frustrated, hard-driving people in a lawless borderland, scuffles were common. "Hundreds of combatants were sometimes seen at fisticuffs, swearing, striking, and gouging, as frontier men only can do those things."[39]

On a sweltering July afternoon, I set out for Auraria, the first town in the nation whose very existence is credited to a gold rush. I wanted to see what remained of the bustling hamlet. I had been expecting some vestige of the village's golden history, perhaps a town layout that whispered through the fog of nearly two centuries and, if I squinted my eyes just right, offered a hazy sketch of this history. Boy, was I wrong.

Auraria today barely rises to the occasion of a ghost town. Auraria is more like the ghost of a memory. Hiding deep within the lush, forested foothills of Georgia's Appalachian Mountains, the town today is a loose collection of buildings that give faint testimony that there was once a town here where men dreamed of riches.

Entering the town from the north, visitors are welcomed by Auraria Church of Almighty God, an ancient oak shading the pure, white exterior of the boxy frame. A cemetery with weathered headstones slopes up a hill toward forest. Nearby, the Auraria Community Club, a thoroughly modern building, sits low-slung and rectangular, shotgun-style, several rooms wide. A wooden sign with images of a pick and shovel reminds readers that Auraria was the "First Gold Rush Town." A portable signboard tells passersby they can rent the venue for special occasions.

Auraria proper is as inconspicuous as its approach. Downtown Auraria, if one can call it that, consists entirely of a T-intersection, which a sign identifies as the "Kate Woody Intersection," in honor of a late local historian. One corner of the intersection is a vacant lot, left to return to nature long ago. Among the growth lies the sole public interpretation of Auraria's legacy, a state roadside historical marker that says the town was "the scene of Georgia's first gold rush," and also claims—incorrectly, as it turns out—that John C. Calhoun gave the town its name.

On the opposite corner lot is a well-kept, story-and-a-half house, its lawn lovingly tended. The property was once home to an alcohol-free tavern run by Grandma Paschal, who collected donations with her son to establish the town's first Baptist church. Now, rising from the shade of a rambling pecan tree, there are yard ornaments: the iron shell of a gazebo, a windmill, a rustic and rusting wagon. While these trinkets likely neither date from nor accurately reflect Auraria's golden age, they are at least a nod to historic affiliation, the way great-grandpa's sword hanging over the fireplace connects a family to a faded past.

Along the intersection's long, unbroken flank sits the singular obvious relic from Auraria's heyday. A boxy general store still stands; its wrinkled and withered clapboard siding still holds off the elements, as does a tin roof so blanketed with old rust it's near crimson. Panes are missing from windows on the gable under the steep pitch of the roof. A weathered sign advertising Coca-Cola hangs from the facade, and on the covered front porch is a Coke machine that hasn't seen service in decades. This building's most recent incarnation was as Woody's General Store, a business that survived until 1982, and the landmark has been stuck in time ever since. But long ago, this was a tavern where gold miners traded their meager earnings for the succor of drink.[40]

To one side of Woody's General Store sits a modern home in need of some TLC, but the question whether the owner of that property also owned Woody's would have to wait; signs made abundantly clear that visitors were not welcome. In an overgrown lot on Woody's opposite flank sits the collapsed Graham Hotel, a compact, two-story structure built in 1826, and a thriving ancillary business during the gold rush. After years of neglect, the hotel collapsed in the early 2000s. Without due attention, that could be the fate of Woody's Store, too.[41]

And that's it: the sum total of downtown Auraria. There's really no designated area to pull off—although I did, into thigh-high weeds, and killed the engine. Auraria today is still and subdued, accompanied by the sound of brush rustled by a soft breeze and birds chirping in the languid Georgia afternoon. Occasionally the rise and fall of a passing car rushed by, the motorist not having reason to stop—not for the historical marker, not for the timeworn trinkets from the town's golden age, not for its ruins. This is a complete 180-degree turn from Auraria of the 1830s, when the town was wild with prospectors and entrepreneurs looking to strike it rich.

Part of the reason Auraria snuffed out was Dahlonega's ascendance to county seat when government officials got around to legally organizing the North Georgia towns that the gold rush created. Dahlonega had a courthouse and other official government institutions, setting it up for permanence that towns like Auraria were not promised. By the 1850s, the easy gold was long gone, and prospectors were leaving for California. Auraria's population dwindled, never again to recover. The town's affair with the craze that named it was intense and colorful, but ultimately fleeting.[42]

Even though there are scant physical clues that testify to Auraria's past, the hills of North Georgia remain marked by the tools that well-financed prospectors employed to coax gold from mountains. Twenty miles northeast of Auraria is Smithgall Woods State Park, a forested expanse of 5,664 acres cut by some of the best trout streams for miles around. A small loop of the park's twenty-eight miles of hiking trails is the Martin's Mine Trail, an easy hike just shy of a mile that carries trekkers through an old mining operation.

As I set out on the trail, I found it hard to imagine that the topography here in the 1890s was a manmade network of cuts, ditches, and tunnels, the work of Scotsman John Martin. "A large 20-stamp mill has been kept running, day and night, working ore," according to one contemporary source. The mine here included three vertical shafts, the deepest descending 125 feet, with a horizontal tunnel connecting them beneath. Deep underground, miners picked and blasted gold-bearing quartz loose. On the surface, that gold ore went to the stamp mill by way of a flume.[43]

The deep shafts closed in on themselves long ago, but their gaping mouths remain, like the open jaw of some yawning skeleton. A mature forest of mixed hardwoods shades this pocked forest floor, and dense stands of rhododendron do their best to obscure the scars. Hard cuts in the sloping terrain remain as reminders of the altered landscape. There are hundreds of such wounds in North Georgia, many on public land, though most others lack the advantage of a well-maintained trail. More still lie on private land. Indeed, these are hardly unique to North Georgia; hard rock mining like this took place all along a gold belt stretching from Georgia through western central Maryland.

The Great Falls unit of the Chesapeake & Ohio Canal National Historical Park, several miles northwest of Washington, DC, contains the remnants of subterranean gold mines worked in the late nineteenth and early twentieth centuries. There, an old, wooden water tower is losing its fight against time and apathy. The changed landscape is hard to miss, even after more than a century.[44]

Virginia, too, is home to its own vivid and quirky golden legacy; none other than Henry Ford once bought a Virginia gold mine, although he was more interested in the heavy equipment than the shiny stuff. The town of Goldvein, Virginia, fifty miles southwest of Washington, DC, is home to the Gold Mining Camp Museum at Monroe Park, which interprets the intense mining activities that occurred at some three hundred mines in the commonwealth beginning in 1906. Outside the interpretive center are two so-called hornet balls—seven-ton, hollow spheres twice as high as a man that were once used to crush ore at an old mine about a mile away.[45]

But in all the east's gold fields, in Virginia and Maryland, in Georgia and the Carolinas, the professional gold diggers are long gone, even though there's still a lot of recoverable gold in the ground: some thirty-three thousand tons nationwide according to the United States Geological Survey. And the gold that's unrecoverable dwarfs this figure, but it's only in trace amounts, locked up in rock.[46]

Yet to this day, out of bedrock occasionally tumbles a nugget that people haven't gotten to. And that's where there are still riches to be had. Not so much in the interpretation of a scarred land and a forgotten history; there's scant interest in interpreting vague holes in the ground and the tumbledown structures that served them. But people, ever eager, will always dream of a lucky find.

Consolidated Gold Mine in Dahlonega, Georgia, was last open for commercial gold mining operations in 1906, but today dozens of people descend into its cramped subterranean passages every day to get a sense of the trek gold miners took all those years ago. I took that journey to the center of the Earth, too, led by a tour guide with shining credentials. Johnny Parker is a world record holder, having taken just 7.52 seconds to reveal eight regulation-sized nuggets in a ten-inch miner's pan filled with an inch of sand. And records are a family matter. Both his wife and daughter are panning champs.[47]

Parker's a joker and doesn't take himself too seriously. "Heeeeere's Johnny!" he said by way of introduction. Parker, goateed with a medium build, sported a felt broad rim hat with gold brooches on it. He wore a gold wedding ring and a gold chain with a huge gold nugget around his neck, a gift from the family that owns Consolidated Gold Mine when he earned the world record.

We descended with a tour group into the ground via the cramped tunnels of the Consolidated underground mine, which is reminiscent of a show cave, irregular passages snaking into the cool bowels of the Earth. Ground water dripped in places as daylight's reach ended, the mine lit by bulbs that throw a dim glow along the path. Jagged rocks held fast to the artificial cavern walls. Parker warned of a protrusion called the wishing rock because if you hit your head, you would wish you hadn't. He pointed out another knot-maker. "This low spot will get your attention real quick," he said. "I used to be six-foot-two."

Consolidated's first run was brief—just eleven years—but intense. Miners used dynamite and drills to remove gold ore from the so-called Glory Hole, a twenty-two-foot-thick vein of gold-laden quartz. Parker fired up a pneumatic drill at a fraction of the power miners once employed against the quartz walls, and the deafening blast clattered onlookers' teeth, stunned us into a natural cringe. Parker silenced the beast, and someone in the group said miners must have been deaf.

"Huh?" Parker replied.[48]

Parker said that the records of Consolidated are lost, but legend holds that fifty-four pounds of pure gold came out of this mine on a single day in its heyday. But as quickly as the glory paid out, it played out, and in the seven-plus decades that the mine was abandoned, it filled with water. The price of gold finally came back up in the 1980s, and a family bought the mine, but it was flooded. Parker helped to restore it. He guessed there are five miles of tunnels, most still muddy and underwater. He said they don't know the extent of them because of the lost records. Some tunnels might snake under a nearby Walmart. "This was like putting together a jigsaw puzzle without seeing the picture."

Now, it's the surface where gold's promise resides. The modern gold panner need not brave dank, damp passages or deafening drills; Consolidated furnishes indoor sluice boxes, clear water running through them and draining with nary a drop spilling out. Bags of sand and gravel can be had without the backbreaking labor of shoveling river bottom. It's all there, and easy, and is as close to the wild gold rush as most people will ever get.

Parker told me to forget what I'd seen on TV. He grabbed a pan and pointed out red lines that had been painted on to show the untutored where to stop. Parker's three-decade quest for gold revealed itself. His rocking motion was more fluid than the water spilling from the pan. He talked of specific gravity and layered sediments, all while teasing tiny flecks of gold from the grit. I inquired about recent finds, and he whipped out his phone, scrolling through the photo gallery. He always puts his booty beside a dime for scale. Some of them would cover a good chunk of FDR's face. Others are much smaller. I asked if he's ever come away with the dream nugget. "I'm still working here, aren't I?" he offered in return.

My take for fifteen minutes of work was a few minuscule flecks of gold, impressive only in that it was more gold than I'd ever found before. But Parker said that for all the worth in the tiny yellow rocks, there's value, too, in the hunt, in the effort. "Everybody has a definition of gold fever," he said. "Gold fever for me is getting to the gold, finding it. Coming away with something is icing on the cake."

Leaving Consolidated, I felt as though I was shortchanging my attempt to penetrate the mist of time without at least getting a small taste of the hardships the twenty-niners endured in those first wild years. For that, I headed ten miles northeast to the small Georgia hamlet of Cleveland and Gold 'n Gem Grubbin', a 150-acre commercial mine that's open to all with gold fever.

The property was once part of the much larger Loud Mine but today offers ore and functioning sluice boxes. Prospectors can purchase buckets containing one of two types of ore mined on-site—that likely to contain gold or that containing gems formed from the same geological processes that made the gold. But it's a third option I went for—panning for gold in Town Creek, a knee-deep stream that runs through the property.[49]

I fetched my pan in Gold 'n Gem Grubbin's office, where I found Brian Devan, who was then co-owner of the mine. Devan was a gold miner for some four decades, including a stint in the wilds of South America. I inquired whether he had any luck down there. "Hell yeah, I did well down there," he said, and gestured to the property around him.

Devan's fifteen minutes of fame came in 2007 when The Travel Channel's show *Cash & Treasures* came calling and he led the host as she hunted Gold 'n Gem Grubbin' ore for a jewelry-worthy amethyst. Like the perky host of that show, explained Devan, many people come expecting a wow-worthy find. And if that's their singular focus, they might leave disappointed. Devan echoed Parker's thoughts, saying the thrill is in the hunt, that the eureka moment of discovery could happen at any time. I asked him for advice as I set off with a pan in hand down to Town Creek. "Don't be fooled by the mica," he said. "It crushes between your fingernails."

I waded into Town Creek, the cool water crystal clear and moving downstream steadily. The difficulties began at once. For one, the Georgia sun was downright oppressive. What's more, walking on an uneven, rock-strewn river bottom is exceedingly difficult and is only made more so by the flowing water.

I declared an arbitrary spot a suitable starting point and bent over to scoop sand and gravel into the pan. I tried to replicate the fluid motion I'd been taught by my tutor Parker, world record holder, but those lessons were long gone, my motions jerky and awkward.

A glimmer of hope appeared when sunlight flickered for an instant off a tiny rock among all the gravel. After a few clunky and unsuccessful attempts to swirl away the sandy gravel, I resorted to poking around with my finger until I saw the glittering rock once more. But no sooner had I removed the suspected fortune than I squeezed it between forefinger and thumbnail. It crumbled. Mica. Fool's gold. Exactly what Devan had warned me about.

And so it went: bend over, scoop pay dirt, swirl incorrectly, find nothing of value, repeat. My back and knees soon began to ache from bending over. My digits all pruned. My skin was slowly roasting in the sun. Bugs discovered me and dove in for the buffet. I found a bucket-sized boulder to sit on, hoping for some relief for my body, now howling in protest of the unfamiliar physical routine. But the sitting helped little, and soon I exhausted all the usable gravel around that perch.

Perhaps it had been an hour, perhaps less, but that was the extent of my gold-panning career. On my final swirl, the familiar glint winked at me, teased me, knowing I was ready to hang up my pan for good. I isolated the tease, and performed the test, by now familiar, knowing full well what would happen. The tiny, shining rock between my fingers was too good to be true, and sure enough, at the slightest pinch, it was gone. Crushed. Just like my dreams of a golden payout.

My way home from North Georgia took me past Cherokee, North Carolina, and I decided to pay a visit to the Eastern Band of Cherokee Indians and their sprawling reservation, a land trust of one hundred square miles called the Qualla Boundary, set deep amid the rolling Great Smoky Mountains of western North Carolina. Broad as the reservation may be, it is just a speck in the territory the Cherokee once occupied, a vast range that today would include significant portions of Alabama, Georgia, South Carolina, North Carolina, Virginia, Kentucky, and Tennessee. This visit was an important reminder that the Appalachian gold rush also altered the region in ways that can't be read in rockfaces.

The story of America's first gold rush is incomplete without acknowledging that the gold belt was the home of the Cherokee and their ancestors for millennia before newcomers arrived. As white and Black Americans began migrating from the coastal lowlands to portions of the rolling terrain of the Appalachian foothills, bringing with them notions of land ownership, they encountered Cherokee Indians, who saw their ancestral lands not as an object that could be deeded, but as a common resource to be shared and stewarded. The parties nurtured a sort of wary peace so long as the newcomers remained the exceptional interloper rather than the aggressor.

But as miners flooded into gold country, there were inevitably encounters between them and the Cherokee, and things escalated. Cherokee people called the influx of gold miners the "Great Intrusion."[50]

National politics were in play, too, and policymakers thought that the land could be better used by white people. Despite efforts by the Cherokee to accede to the demands of an increasingly agitated ruling class, they found little that would satisfy firebrands like Andrew Jackson. The Indian Removal Act of 1830, enacted at the height of the Georgia gold rush, set the stage for the Trail of Tears. American soldiers and militiamen forced some twenty thousand Cherokee to endure a brutal march to designated lands west of the Mississippi River. Along the way, facing starvation and freezing temperatures, more than four thousand of the refugees died.[51]

But not all of the Cherokee left. Several hundred stayed behind. Some evaded the authorities. Others struck deals to remain in place. The Eastern Band descend from those who stayed. About two-thirds of the tribe's fourteen thousand members live in the Qualla Boundary. Visitors to this land today find Cherokee culture thriving, with street signs both in English and in the Cherokee syllabary of their native language. On summer days Cherokee dancers invite onlookers to participate in cultural rituals in the street. The Museum of the Cherokee Indian and Oconaluftee Indian Village, a living history museum staffed by Cherokee, preserve the ancient ways and wisdom. Qualla Arts and Crafts Mutual offers handmade baskets, jewelry, and sculpture.[52]

After the Trail of Tears, the Eastern Band repopulated and reorganized, gained federal recognition, and, with the weight of their organization, found financial assistance. Gold fever among outsiders may have helped set in motion the forced removal of Cherokee people. Gold fever now brings outsiders back.

Motorists who round a bend on US Highway 19, the main east–west corridor through the Qualla Boundary, see a looming edifice storm into view. Harrah's Cherokee Casino Resort is a twenty-one-story behemoth that rises from the rolling hills of the reservation like a monument. The complex, opened in 1997, has 150,000 square feet of gaming space and eleven hundred hotel rooms.[53]

So successful was the Eastern Band's foray into gaming that they opened an additional casino fifty miles southwest off the Qualla Boundary. And the tribe broke ground in 2018 to expand those accommodations by more than half and quintuple the size of its convention center. The casinos employ 3,600 people, hundreds of whom are Cherokee, and bring in annual profits of three hundred million dollars. The tribe shares this wealth with members in what's termed "per capita payments." Every man, woman, and child currently receives roughly ten to fourteen thousand dollars in twice-annual payments.[54]

And much of this is because people, by their very nature, will never stop looking for easy money. But whether in a gold rush or in a casino, many more people lose than win. The Eastern Band, however, has discovered a critical secret that's a timeless recipe for success: own the mine, and people will always come chasing golden dreams.

Chapter 3

Civil War Earthworks: What's Left When War Hits Home

May 20, 1864, was a bad day for Confederate Brigadier General William S. Walker. That afternoon, he led an attack against a line of earthworks near Chester, Virginia, that had been going back and forth between the Union and Confederate forces for several hours.

The dense woods were still smoldering after being intentionally lit ablaze by Rebels wanting to conceal their movements. The scene was disorienting. Walker soon realized that he and his command were in a tight spot. He was new to the surroundings and didn't have a good handle on the terrain, so he rode around the unfamiliar ground on his horse trying to make sense of everything and figure out what to do next.

Walker got turned around in the young pines and emerged alone in a clearing staring at the muzzles of Company C of the Sixty-Seventh Ohio Volunteer Infantry—enemy soldiers who occupied the very earthworks he had orders to retake. The Yanks shouted for Walker to surrender. Realizing he was in a bit of a pickle, Walker first tried a ruse. "Hold your position firmly, boys, and I will ride back for reinforcements, and we will drive these Rebels to hell," he barked, pretending to be a Union commander.

The rank-and-file weren't buying the Yankee officer bit, though. Perhaps it was that Walker was dressed in a dashing Confederate uniform. So he hatched a more conventional plan B and turned tail, but the prospect of killing Rebel brass was too tempting for the Ohioans. They let fly a volley of musket fire. Three bullets hit Walker. Sixteen hit his horse.

Walker's wounds were grievous. Nobody really expected him to live, not even Walker himself. "Let me rest somewhere and dictate some last words to my wife and commander," he gasped as Union soldiers carried him from the field. A surgeon amputated Walker's leg later that night by the flickering light of a bonfire. To everyone's astonishment, Walker not only lived but returned to active service later that year after being exchanged for a Union officer who'd also had his leg cut off.[55]

A century and a half later, I met George Fickett one chilly winter morning near the very spot Walker fell. I ordered a sausage biscuit combo with sweet tea.

The trenches Walker took three bullets for never had a chance. They intersected a major east–west corridor, now Virginia State Route 10, on the Bermuda Hundred peninsula near Richmond. The spot where Walker stared down the muzzles of a company's worth of muskets is now an intersection with eleven lanes.

I met Fickett because he, like other men before him, had come to Bermuda Hundred for a noble cause. But his is a more modern mission: to preserve what's left of the trenches that Walker and so many other soldiers were willing to die for. Even though servicemen dug hundreds of miles of earthworks during the Civil War, they are now an endangered national treasure.

Trenches ringed the dueling capitals of Richmond and Washington, DC. They snaked across far-flung reaches of the Virginia countryside. Tennessee, Mississippi, South Carolina, and Georgia all had their fair share. From the hills north of Atlanta, General William T. Sherman cabled superiors: "The whole country is one vast fort," he described. Confederates "have at least fifty miles of connected trenches." Earthworks laced the landscape on Union soil, too, in Washington, DC; Maryland; Pennsylvania; Kentucky; and Missouri.[56]

In the one hundred sixty years since soldiers carved these defenses from the land, time and growth have been merciless grim reapers. There's no definitive estimate of how many Civil War earthworks have been lost in some manner—paved over, plowed under, flattened to the surrounding grade. But the vast majority, in the ninety-plus-percent range according to the best educated guesses, are history.

Of course, there are long lines of well-preserved trenches at familiar Civil War battlefields—Vicksburg, Spotsylvania, and Cold

Harbor, to name a few. Still, those are just a small fraction of the earthworks soldiers made. The remaining lines lace the suburbs and countryside, across fields, in stands of timber, and in backyards, never having been given special protection, their fate subject to whims of circumstance—a tight spot for irreplaceable relics.

When Union Army veteran and Boston journalist Russell H. Conwell visited Cold Harbor, Virginia, four years after the battle there, he happened upon a disturbing scene. A man had exhumed from the earthworks the uniformed remains of a Massachusetts artillerist with a bullet hole through his skull. The dead serviceman wasn't as worrisome to Conwell as was the reason he'd been dug up—for any valuables there with him. Sure enough, a silver watch was among the soldier's effects. Conwell bought the watch off the scavenger and sent it back to Boston hoping someone might identify it.[57]

Conwell's discovery wasn't out-of-the-ordinary; he witnessed a similar exhumation later that day. Neither was the scavenger some callous renegade. When the fighting stopped, hordes of people descended on the Civil War's deserted trenches with the same thought in mind: payday. All those untold miles of earthworks weren't an object of reverence for the people who lived among a landscape and economy crippled by four years of war. The dirt, heaped in long mounds, was in the way of a return to some semblance of normalcy and there was little reason for anyone to bother with preserving them.

Earthworks were never meant to be long-term defenses to begin with. At the most fundamental level, they consisted of two parts: a ditch, created when soldiers excavated earth, and a parapet, created by mounding the dirt. The ditch could be on either or both sides of the parapet. Some Civil War earthworks got pretty elaborate with sharp angles, tunnels, and bomb shelters, as well as obstacles like felled trees or telegraph wire, depending on how long armies anticipated staying there. Soldiers called them all sorts of names: earthworks, breastworks, entrenchments. Whatever the moniker, their function was short-term; Dennis Hart Mahan, the US Army officer who wrote the book on earthworks, called them "Temporary or Field Fortifications."[58]

Some earthworks represented massive efforts in planning and maintenance, as with the sixty-eight enclosed forts, ninety-three batteries, and twenty miles of trenches around Washington, DC. Oftentimes, though, soldiers dug earthworks hastily because not doing so exposed life and limb to all the hot lead enemy soldiers were happy to share.

Digging earthworks was as familiar to Civil War soldiers as hardtack and head lice. Sergeant Samuel Clear of the 116th Pennsylvania described in his diary, while plodding through the Virginia countryside in 1864, how often soldiers dug in: "Marched one mile into a wheat field and threw up breastworks," he wrote on May 21st. Then after a brief skirmish compelled them to move on May 23rd: "We are entrenching and so are the enemy." On the 28th, his regiment "went one mile, threw up works." The next day they "moved again and threw up new works, finished late in the night." And the next: "moved a half mile and threw up new works." And the next: "short advance, under heavy fire, threw up new works."[59]

Soldiers hoped for spades, picks, and shovels to help them, but often used whatever was at their disposal—knives, plates, cups, their hands—in order to get something between them and certain death. And when they weren't digging, or moving, or fighting over these trenches, they languished there, exposed to the elements. "Lying in the trenches all day & night," wrote Pennsylvania Sergeant M.L. Gordon on May 18, 1864, at Bermuda Hundred. "Lay in the trenches all last night," he began an entry two days later. The terse double entry for May 24th and 25th: "Nothing important. Lie in the trenches every night."[60]

When the sun shined, soldiers huddled under tent canvases or blankets to escape its brutal rays. When rain poured, the ditches filled and turned into a sanitary nightmare, in large part because of all the unwashed men whose olfactory essence ripened in the elements. "Our shirts from sweat and grime had gotten so dirty and stiff they would almost stand upright," recalled the Fifty-Sixth North Carolina's Private James Elliott, who occupied the trenches opposite M.L. Gordon.[61]

After the war, veterans' groups sometimes reunited at fortifications, and in at least one case even bought a swath of trenches where they'd served for a time, but there was little reason to protect the miles and miles of trenches that soldiers had made during the war. Most just weren't that fond a memory.[62]

For the Southern property owners, the trenches lost any sentimentality at once. "Three and a half years I played soldier," wrote a testy Confederate veteran to *The Daily State Journal* of Richmond in 1873, "and when I returned my farm was badly cut up and disfigured with breastworks; my wood all cut down and carried off." The writer didn't mince words. He now called Virginia—the commonwealth he'd been willing to die for—a "heartless, bloody robber."[63]

For some former Confederates, the earthworks that stretched across the southern states were a monument to their loss. John T. Trowbridge, like Conwell, was a Bostonian sent South after the war to compile a narrative on the state of the defeated Confederacy. Near Spotsylvania, the scene of bloody fighting from May 8 to 21, 1864, Trowbridge and a guide happened upon a former Confederate soldier who learned their destination was the battlefield. Immediately, the man pegged Trowbridge for a northerner. Trowbridge asked how the veteran knew. "Because no South'n man ever goes to the battlefields," he said, "we've seen enough of 'em."[64]

Even for Union sympathizers near Washington, DC, the forts protecting the city had come at a dear price; virtually all the ground they'd been erected on was confiscated then returned to them years later in no condition to be of any use. There was little reason to keep earthworks around.[65]

As Conwell had observed, self-styled miners dug through earthworks for profit; they could sell metal for scrap and take horse remains to bone grinders who would pulverize them for fertilizer. People took forts' hardware such as wood and occasional metal, even moved into bomb shelters armies had constructed as part of the fortifications. Farmers had no use for trenches—they reduced their amount of tillable acreage, and, thus, profits—so they plowed earthworks to ground level.[66]

Nevertheless, so common were earthworks that miners and farmers couldn't flatten all of them—not by a long shot. Many miles of trenches were left where they lay and became fertile ground for pioneer grasses and shrubs that found and thrived on the naked soil.

"Rebel forts overgrown with weeds," Trowbridge wrote of the works he saw at Manassas Junction in 1865. At Cold Harbor in 1866, Theodore Lyman, a Union officer who toured the South, saw boys catching eels in earthworks near the Chickahominy River that were flooded with water, "which shows how soon fish get into new water!" he wrote. The "growth of underbrush" was among the reasons Conwell and his companions couldn't recognize much at the Big Bethel battlefield eight years after the fighting there.[67]

Given enough time, all the scrubby weeds and underbrush gave way to tall stands of trees. A *Philadelphia Times* correspondent toured the Wilderness battlefield in August 1881, fifteen years after the fighting there. He and a local guide came to a new growth of pines some twenty or thirty feet tall which, at the time of the battle, "was an open field and through it ran a ditch. The ditch remains, but its bed is dry and overgrown with weeds."[68]

As destructive as all that growth seems, however, it turns out that, in terms of long-term preservation, vegetation was the best thing that could have happened to the trenches, because the enemy that will one day level even the most protected earthworks isn't what grows up from ground level, but what falls from the sky.

Rain poses two problems for earthworks. The first is the collapse of soil particles that occurs when the water impacts the soil. This includes not only those drops that fall directly from the sky, but also those that consolidate on leaves and stems in the forest canopy and then plunge with a heavier humph, breaking away more and larger chunks of soil. This has the potential to happen millions of times on a single rainy day. Also, water that is pulled by gravity down sloping ground picks up any loose particles of soil and deposits them downhill. On a trench that's mostly dirt, the rain will move earth from the parapet to the ditch, and the two extremes in elevation will get closer over time.

A mature forest atop the earthworks is the most effective deterrent against erosion. A dense overstory in the canopy, a brushy understory near ground level, and a thick blanket of leaf litter on the ground—these all but eliminate the threat that water will move dirt. In addition to blocking raindrops' jarring impact, the spongy texture and rough features that old growth imparts in the ground enables the soil to better absorb the rainwater, rather than siphoning it downhill along with any particles it contains.[69]

But earthworks that were protected from the elements had other problems to contend with. As the country's population grew, earthworks would be leveled to make space for new development.

Russell Conwell, the northern correspondent, was among the first writers to mourn the destruction of earthworks for development. He lamented in 1869 that the Georgetown Heights neighborhood of Washington, DC, site of a Union garrison during the war, was "now becoming most fashionable for the residences of the rich." In time there'd be a long line of preservationists behind Conwell, because the rapid growth the nation encountered after the Civil War collided with the burgeoning notion that maybe keeping some of those earthworks around was a way to honor soldiers' sacrifices. Thus launched a tricky and enduring engagement between advocates of private property rights and historic preservation.[70]

When Civil War soldiers constructed earthworks to defend the Union and Confederate capitals, they did so outside the perimeter of the cities' densely inhabited streets. Each city encountered a postwar population boom, however, that turned what was once rural fringe into prime suburban real estate. In instance after instance, earthworks disappeared to make way for construction or other civil engineering projects.

Preservationists' demands that the government step in was an uphill battle, but eventually paid off. Congress appropriated funds to buy or retain ownership of eighteen of Washington, DC's Civil War forts and batteries in the 1920s and battlefields around Richmond in 1929. Still, most of the earthworks that had managed to make it to the twentieth century weren't protected in any formal sense. They were on private property.[71]

Meanwhile, the further people got from the Civil War, the weaker a connection they had to it, even if trenches still crisscrossed the countryside. When it came time to decide whether to build on a parcel that contained earthworks, it was hard to justify saving overgrown, old trenches when there were others like them just down the road, some of which were under the protection of the federal government.

For much of the twentieth century, landowners might have built around earthworks if density wasn't especially heavy or site plans were flexible, which is why earthworks lay silently in suburbs amid neighborhoods and apartment complexes. Trenches that stood in the way of larger plans or higher density, though, forced public officials and preservationists into uncomfortable dances, as in Mechanicsville, Virginia, in 1990.

After a long career in agriculture, Oscar Via Jr. decided to retire and sell the old homestead to a developer. The farm was his nest egg. Suburban Richmond was getting closer by the year. He had a willing buyer. And then, a hitch: his land contained a long line of Civil War earthworks, and the county planning commission recommended ninety-five percent of them be preserved as a developer transformed the property into an eight-hundred-home golf course community. Via was incensed. He saw years of red tape, the deal slipping through his fingers, so he simply eliminated the sticking point. He hired a bulldozer crew, which leveled about half of the one thousand linear feet of trenches and would have finished the job had the dozer not thrown a track.

Via's action cleaved the community. Preservationists called him a cultural terrorist. Businessmen hailed him as a hero of private property rights. Whatever Via was, his actions raised questions about whether Americans can reconcile their reverence for private property rights with their responsibility to historic resources. After a long and heated community conversation, the development on Via's land proceeded. Via died in 2001, but today, in the woods of Mechanicsville's Pebble Creek neighborhood, is a line of Civil War earthworks that ends abruptly.[72]

Most instances of disappearing earthworks didn't garner the type of publicity of the Via tract. They vanished anonymously as property changed hands, businesses and roads expanded, and loggers thinned wooded tracts. Earthworks are the last physical trace left by Civil War soldiers in the field, and they're fading. Right after the war, people could see the stumps of trees cut down by musket fire. Fifteen years later, rusty and rotten relics still littered the ground where soldiers once marched. Today, though, even the longest-lived footprints have disappeared—disintegrated, carted off, buried. All of them, that is, except one. The only things left on the land itself are earthworks. And now that last tangible link to a war fought on the very ground beneath our feet is threatened.

That's where George Fickett comes in. He's taken it upon himself to save forgotten trenches in one corner of Virginia where competing obligations to free enterprise and historic preservation are coming to a head. Fickett has found a way to enlist unexpected supporters: landowners, developers, and civil engineers, many of whom often have competing visions for land use.

My meeting with Fickett for a bite to eat at the Hardee's near where General Walker took a few Minié balls was the beginning of a tour he gave me of Bermuda Hundred's extensive earthworks.

Fickett is stocky and no-nonsense: a silver-haired baby boomer who rides a Harley. Once you get him talking, especially about the Civil War, it's hard to get a word in edgewise. He works as a geographic information systems (GIS) specialist for the local government of Chesterfield County, Virginia, using computer software to update local maps as the rapidly growing suburb of Richmond adds new roads and subdivisions.

Fickett's upbringing in nearby Prince George County, itself amply carved with earthworks, had a strong bearing on who he became as an adult. As a teenager in the 1960s, he saw the destruction of local landmarks such as Fort Sedgwick, a fort also known as Fort Hell that figured prominently in the Siege of Petersburg. "Civil War sites were being destroyed so fast then," Fickett told me. "That really moved me. Later on, in my thirties, I realized with my job in Chesterfield County I had a chance to do something about it. So when I saw an opportunity to save a site, I invested my time to make it happen."

Today the Bermuda Hundred peninsula, formed by the confluence of the James and Appomattox Rivers, has an industrial corridor of trucking terminals, heavy equipment suppliers, and commuters' hotels. Route 10 bisects residential lots and, increasingly, suburban neighborhoods. A hundred fifty years ago, however, Bermuda Hundred was rural and agricultural, ten long miles from the Union Army's juiciest prize: Richmond. General Ulysses S. Grant realized how ideally suited the Bermuda Hundred peninsula was for threatening Richmond from the southeast, so in 1864 he sent the bald, droopy-jowled Major General Benjamin Butler and thirty-three thousand Union soldiers to do just that.

Confederates got there first, and eighteen thousand Rebels under General P. G. T. Beauregard plugged the hole. After a couple weeks of on-again, off-again heavy skirmishing (including the Battle of Ware Bottom Church, where General Walker fell), the adversaries fortified their positions across the breadth of the peninsula. The Yankees constructed a two-and-a-half-mile line of earthworks across the peninsula's narrowest point, and the Rebels developed a three-and-a-half-mile string they called the Howlett Line just west of their bottled-up enemy.[73]

"There are earthworks literally all across this peninsula," Fickett told me as we peeled off in his Ford F-150 down a timeworn side street. He ticked off the unexpected places where 150-year-old trenches and rifle pits sat alongside modern development: backyards, parking lots, playgrounds, the shoulder of Route 10, an Interstate 95 exit cloverleaf. "You just have to know where to look for them," he said.

Of all people, Fickett is the person who knows where they are on Bermuda Hundred. He has invested more than three decades in these forgotten trenches. I was incredulous at his claim of ubiquitous earthworks given all the trappings of industry about. No sooner had I opened my mouth to share my doubts, though, than we arrived at Parker's Battery, a wooded and well-preserved stretch of the Howlett Line that appeared seemingly out of nowhere. We parked and walked around some. High voltage power lines loomed overhead. A freight train lumbered by on the tracks maybe fifty yards in front of the earthworks, blaring its ear-splitting horn. Fickett explained how the National Park Service reopened this tract after serious preservation efforts began on Bermuda Hundred in the 1960s.

Back in the truck, the roads became more reminiscent of Bermuda Hundred before the twentieth century appeared, woodsier and more rustic. Away from heavy development, the trenches assumed a different persona, too. They lengthened and rambled, and every little stretch took on a bit of character.

Fickett slowed his truck and pointed off into a patch of mature trees. "Look there. See it? Ten, fifteen yards in? That's part of the Howlett Line," he said. A soft trench came out of the woods to the edge of the road, briefly announcing its existence before retreating again into the dense vegetation. Fickett continued driving, slowing each time the earthworks would be visible from the truck. Bouncing along Bermuda Hundred's back roads, I saw trenches topped by tumbledown chain-link fences, driveways with rifle pits on either side, forts in suburban developments. They were, as Fickett had claimed, everywhere.

Along narrow rural roads we passed a couple lots where heavy machinery had graded a building site, exposing the layer of bright orange clay under the topsoil. "Hmm." Fickett stared awhile at the disturbance. "That's new."

Bermuda Hundred has grown around these earthworks without much regard for their existence. The trenches' identity and the connection they have to the people who live on them have been lost along the way. Long ago it was said that there was the same hatred on this peninsula for Union General Benjamin Butler as there was for General William T. Sherman in the parts of Georgia and South Carolina his troops ravaged. You'd be hard-pressed today to find a Chesterfield local who could tell you who Butler was.

It took a lot of work to get people excited about faded old trenches that had been there as long as anyone could remember, but Fickett did it—numerous times. Because he's discovered that the key to saving what remains of Civil War earthworks is not to stand in the way of progress, but to work with it.

"Development is inevitable," said Fickett. For Bermuda Hundred, a building growth spurt came when Interstate 295, a speedy bypass around Richmond, opened in 1992. Residential and commercial development skyrocketed then and hasn't let up since. "The key is knowledge. When the landowner knows there is a historic site on the property, we have a better chance of saving it. I saw the vision for this years ago, but I knew I'd need help—that I couldn't do it on my own," he said. Fickett reached out to Scott Williams, who is also a member of the Chesterfield Historical Society and works for Chesterfield County's municipal government. "Scott has better technical know-how, and I know where the earthworks are."

Fickett's secret isn't all that complicated; he's just mapping the earthworks and making that information available to other planning and development professionals. He began with an old map, one that the US Army Corps of Engineers made after surveying the peninsula's extensive earthworks in 1867. "We digitized that into Chesterfield County's map database," he said. "Then we geo-referenced that on known points."

So if Fickett knew, for example, that a particular bend in the trenches indicated on the map matched up with an identical feature in the earthworks that exists on the ground, he was able to roughly synchronize old and new maps. But he still had a lot of work to do, because the 1867 map was a good approximation, but just that—an approximation, made with nineteenth-century technology. Fickett and Williams brought the twenty-first century on board. "We took portable GPS units into the field, found the trenches in the places the maps said they should be, gathered coordinates, then put those numbers into the county database."

Their first target was the three-and-a-half-mile-long main body of the Howlett Line. That stretch took them all day. "A lot of it was on flat or open ground, but some of it was down ravines, through brambles and thickets. A lot of curious landowners would come out and want to talk to us. They were very interested in what we were doing. We tried to be nice and have a conversation, but the more we did that, the more GPS time we lost."

Another thing that contributed to the difficulty of mapping the Howlett Line is that much of it is long gone. For that, Fickett had another tool at his disposal: historic aerial photography, made in the 1930s to survey agricultural lands. Those grainy images were helpful; disturbed earth and shadows cast by parapets stood in sharp relief on an otherwise unremarkable field when seen in black and white from the sky. Stretches of the Howlett Line that were lost years back got verified points on the map despite that they were under a warehouse, parking lot, or jungle gym.

What's come of all this legwork is a master map of Chesterfield's earthworks. These aren't good guesses or rough sketches; they're hyper-accurate depictions of where the earthworks are or once were. The thin lines on Chesterfield's map make abrupt turns and have sharp angles. They clip suburban back yards at the end of cul-de-sacs by a few feet. They have what appear to be whiskers and cross over all of Bermuda Hundred's thoroughfares.

The map isn't publicly available out of respect for the privacy of property owners; some might be happy to acknowledge that their land contains, or once contained, earthworks, but most would rather just not make that known. The earthworks map is accessible, however, to county departments and landowners who want to build—be it an addition to a house or a hundred-plus-home development.

In planning and engineering reviews, county officials can advise the landowner that there are historic resources on the land. That knowledge is critical to saving earthworks because it allows engineers and architects to plan around the trenches from square one. Landowners are more or less free to do with their property what they choose—including flattening earthworks if they're so inclined. But ever since this county earthworks map has been around, landowners have often been willing to set aside sensitive property rather than pave over it.

It helps that Fickett is a realist when it comes to what can be saved and acknowledges that property owners have rights, too. "Not every little rifle pit needs to be preserved," he said. As a county employee, he catches wind of building plans early on and engages in low-pressure dialogue to make sure that all parties involved reap benefits: the developer, the county, and the history that's being saved. There's always some give and take, but Fickett's goal is to make sure that everyone feels like they've gained something in the end.

For instance, Fickett worked with developer Lawson Chenoweth before the sprawling Ramblewood Forest neighborhood began to take shape. Chenoweth donated 11.7 acres of land as a substitute for part of the required proffers, or money the developer pays the county for the new roads, schools, and services those new homes will require. That parcel, which contains fifteen hundred linear feet of Union earthworks, became Sergeant James Engle Park, named for a Union soldier who won the Medal of Honor on that spot for extraordinary heroism when he carried ammunition to pickets far in front of the main Union line under heavy enemy fire.

There's no telling how James Engle would have felt about the place where he earned the nation's highest military honor backing up to suburban back yards. He might have said that was what he was fighting for: the freedom of all Americans to grow and build and live how they pleased. Or he might have preferred that it not be ground for Fido's daily constitutional. But at least there remains a patch of physical evidence embodying his and other servicemen's struggles, there for all to enjoy, to ponder what might have compelled him to leave those trenches and deliver ammunition to his comrades-in-arms.[74]

Fickett is not the only one using GPS technology to map earthworks. The National Park Service, for instance, has long since mapped earthworks on federal property. Other counties rich in Civil War fortifications have likewise seen some efforts to map and catalog their historic resources on the land. But Fickett seems to have found the perfect spot to place that information: at the municipal government level, the portal through which all development must go before the first bulldozer sputters to life.[75]

And that's a complete about-face that Fickett has witnessed in his tenure with the county. "In the 1980s, I was beating my head against the wall because people didn't care: about the Civil War, about earthworks, about preservation. In the seventies and eighties, the first indication that an earthwork was going to be destroyed was the bulldozer rolling off the truck."

Despite the fact that Bermuda Hundred will always play second fiddle to the war's bigger battles, Fickett remains undaunted. This, he feels, is a calling, a worthy avocation, and he's uniquely situated with the tools and expertise to honor the sacrifices that men made there so long ago. "Bermuda Hundred may not be as well-known as other places, but this is still ground that men fought and died for. And it's worth saving what we can for nothing more than that," Fickett said.

All the earthworks will melt into the earth eventually. Even under the best of conditions—a mature forest dropping copious leaf litter—earthworks erode at the rate of about 150 tons of earth per surface acre annually.[76]

The people who come in direct contact with earthworks, such

as landowners and developers, mostly seem to agree that the effort to rescue them from obscurity, to make them known again after a long dormancy, is worthwhile. It's like cataloging a species known to be going extinct. For all the effort soldiers expended digging these trenches, for all the unknown graves scattered around them, for the miles and miles of earthworks that were flattened for progress, keeping what's left is the least we can do.

Back during the Civil War, it was common for the relatives of a deceased person, particularly a soldier, to take some memento of their loved one, some physical reminder of his life and last days, some proof of his death—a swatch of cloth, for instance, or a lock of hair.[77]

For the vast majority of Civil War veterans—that's nearly three million men (and many women)—all physical traces, save a lonely, weathered headstone, are gone, taken by time and the elements. The earthworks that stretch across the changing landscape are those soldiers' silent testament, the only relic we have remaining for some of them. Preserving that last link, the last shadow of their work, is the closest we can get as a culture, as a community, to keeping a piece of them. They might not have ever expected those holes they dug to be so precious, but they'd probably be happy to see us keeping them around.

Chapter 4

Tide Mills: The Forgotten Art of Trapping Lunar Energy

Slade's Mill should have tumbled into the marsh long ago. For three centuries, the building weathered all sorts of hazards—fires and floods, a tornado, even a direct hit from a car careening out of control on ice. But the noble old soul still stands, sustained by the water that ebbs and flows beneath it every day without fail.

That constant wash is Slade's Mill's raison d'être. The structure is a rare survivor from a class of buildings called tide mills. Today the water around it is a selling point. A third of the cedar-shingle-sided building sits on pilings directly over Mill Creek, in a short stretch of undeveloped bank along an otherwise industrial shoreline.

Now known as Slade's Mill Apartments, its residents appreciate their waterfront views. They name the geese who call this stretch home and watch as the flowing tide makes eddies that swirl around the pilings. But centuries ago, people valued that same position for another reason altogether: power. Free-flowing energy to be harnessed and used. So here, on a thin, tidal ribbon separating the Greater Boston communities of Revere and Chelsea, an enterprising colonist built a power plant four decades before Americans began their struggle for independence from Great Britain.[78]

Admittedly, it's a challenge to get the general population jazzed about old-timey mills. The world is peppered with the now-rickety shacks that once powered our ancestors' lives. More than a few are painstakingly preserved along country byways, the prides of local historical societies. But the vast majority of the survivors are wind and watermills. There are few tide mills like Slade's—maybe a dozen or so left in North America, none of which are operable. Once ubiquitous along America's East Coast, tide mills now flirt with extinction. The hazards that Slade's has survived through the years have claimed hundreds of others.[79]

Most folks might shrug off tide mills' disappearance; they're obsolete and demand the type of attention and funding that's hard to come by even in good years. But each time a tide mill slips into oblivion, we don't just surrender some dusty old relic that causes docents' hearts to skip a beat. We also loosen a tenuous connection to the natural world.

Consider that we have already lost much of that connection. Ground beef comes from a package, not an animal. Weather holds little sway on our routines as we scurry from air-conditioned automobile to air-conditioned office. And no longer do tides, when they're noticed at all, wield power and influence over our lives. Very few people today plan travel or workdays around them.

In our haste to insulate ourselves from nature's inconveniences, we've lost perspectives along the way. We've cut a thousand small ties with the natural world until all of a sudden, we're apart from nature rather than a part of it. I set out to gauge the strength of one of those frayed cords—the last of the remaining tide mills. And it turns out the last leg isn't quite what I expected it to be.

Like their quarry, tide mill enthusiasts are a quirky lot: getting on in years, mostly, but stalwart and resolute. John Goff is one of them. Until his recent retirement, Goff was a preservation and restoration architect who worked from his Salem, Massachusetts, home, a nineteenth-century Federal with wear and tear he attributed to an obsession with historic architecture. Goff can point out the exact spot along one of Salem's main streets where a devastating fire in 1914 stopped burning, how homes north of Leach Street are distinctly different from those to the south.

He can talk all day on old architecture with an earnest and engaging admiration. His passion for design, particularly that of mills, was cultivated at an early age. He grew up near Winnegance, Maine, a town that once had eight sawmills powered by tidewater. Even though the nineteenth century mills had long since burned down by the time Goff came along, his family lived in the house of the complex's owner. The woodwork, he remembers, was exquisite. Other nearby homes to this day stand tall and are made of the Maine virgin hardwoods that went through Winnegance's mills.

A fortuitous bathroom break clinched his lifelong appreciation for tide mills. When Goff was a young adult and his now-grown-up daughter was a bundle of joy, he pulled over in Kennebunkport to change her diaper during a road trip to the old family place in Maine. That pitstop, however, happened to be right at a tide mill, which he noted with some admiration and made plans to revisit. A month later, though, the mill burned to the ground. He poked through the rubble afterward, finding some of the mill's hardware, but lamented the lost opportunity.

That loss spurred him to find other tide mills and record information about them before they, too, burned, fell, or otherwise blinked off the map. Now, if there's anyone, anywhere who gets excited about tide mills, it's Goff. He gives lectures and organizes conferences. He's a member of the Tide Mill Institute, the only group in the country devoted exclusively to the preservation of tide mills at large. When I met Goff at his home office on a bright August morning, we set off in search of several of the country's last tide mills with a binder-full of historical data he had compiled.

Even besides Greater Boston's notoriously nasty traffic, accessing Slade's Mill was challenging. A couple illegal U-turns after spotting the mill, we turned into the small parking lot tucked between the Chelsea River and the four-lane road. A tornado, of all things, had blown through Revere the week before. All in all, the mill seemed to have weathered the unusual event well. It is, after all, a colossus of a building: three stories high and as wide as a short city block, with a third of its mass perched on pilings over Mill Creek. The old mill now contains seventeen studio and one-bedroom apartments as well as a first-floor common area. Asphalt shingles had blown off the roof, leaving patches of exposed tarpaper. Other than that, the old mill looked more or less intact.

The property manager was on-site and happy to have us look around but apologized for not being able to help; he was buried in work orders thanks to the tornado. The mill's first floor was a classy and historic lobby adorned with mill-related hardware: shipping crates and old signage, the wood worn smooth, humming deep hues of aged and trodden timber. The building's deed requires this be opened for tours by appointment, but these days few people bother, which is surprising, given how ubiquitous its products once were. Goff and I lifted the lid on a long crate of a contraption, and the smell blew over us at once: cardamom. This had been where a screw shaft pushed milled spice into tins. Mustard-colored residue still lined the box a half-century later.

If you can't place Slade's Mill, think of Grandma's spice cabinet. D&L Slade Company was New England's largest spice manufacturer for much of the nineteenth and twentieth centuries. Slade's Spices made their way around the world, as far as Asia, and until 1932, the juice that powered this mill rose and fell underneath it, every day, on schedule.[80]

Slade's and other tide mills harnessed the power of tides by trapping high water then releasing it all at once. Millers accomplished this by building an earthen berm across a tidal creek—in the case of Slade's Mill, the headwaters of the Chelsea River—and installing a set of tide gates at an opening. Millers would open the gates to flood the millpond when the tide came in then close them to keep the water there. When the tide on the opposite side was low, the miller opened the gates, allowing the rushing water to flow out through the narrow opening over a wheel, transforming all that potential energy into motion.[81]

The higher the tides, the more energy one could extract. Tide mills were particularly potent in Maine and other coastal areas where the difference between high tide and low was as much as ten feet.[82]

Of course, tide milling had a downside. Tides are caused by the gravity of the moon tugging on the Earth's bodies of water. It pulls and distorts them just enough to make a few feet of difference at sea level. Because the moon's orbit doesn't exactly sync up with the Earth's twenty-four-hour day, however, the timing of the tides changes a little each day. If high water comes today at 10:40, tomorrow it's going to be somewhere around 11:40. So the window for work is always a moving target.[83]

Outside, Goff and I looked for ways to access Slade Mill's underbelly, at least the half of it sitting on pilings over Mill Creek. We wanted to see what remained, to check for any pre-1937 hardware that had, against all odds, stuck it out all these years. He thought that basic instruction on tide mills might be a little easier with real-life visual aids. But no dice. What we found instead was a poignant vista that painted a full circle.

Through those pilings holding up the southern third of Slade's Mill flowed tidewater out of Mill Creek into the Chelsea River, and a shoreline studded with hundreds of years of man's influence: the rotten trunks of old pilings, riprap, and litter. A short distance downstream, the water swept the banks of an area heavy with the aging brick skeleton of some industrial enterprise, and a long-dormant smokestack—and beside that shuttered plant, a twenty-first century windmill, its sleek blades sitting idly against a feeble breeze. "Look at what we have here," Goff said, sweeping his view. "You have eighteenth and nineteenth centuries meets twentieth and twenty-first."

We bid adieu to Slade's Mill, got in the car, and slipped into the stream of traffic. As Goff adroitly navigated Greater Boston's frenetic streets, he pointed out the traces of energy's past that have long since been forgotten: a filled and paved site near Mill Street and Pond Street in Salem, a French millstone that lies flat as a sidewalk ornament, traversed by hundreds of pedestrians daily.

But what Goff really wanted to show me sat languishing beneath Elliott Street in Beverly. We parked at a McDonald's and climbed our way down the bank beside it to a culvert through which flowed the last of an ebb tide. Rotten pilings and vertical sheathing are all that are left of the oldest corn mill in Beverly, The mucky tidal flat in front of the place the mill once stood was flecked with the detritus of an urban waterway: plastic bottles, bags, a shopping cart. The steep bank was littered with tons and tons of what appeared to be slag.[84]

This is what became of hundreds of tide mills, and even remnants like these are rare. Goff stepped into the spongy mud, good shoes and all, snapping photographs from all sorts of angles. This was a rare chance, the death throes of an irretrievable slice of history. "This is only visible at low tide, as in now," he said. "I've told a lot of people they should do some sort of archaeological work out here, at least document it before it's totally gone."

Long ago, the Bass River in front of this mill was ship-deep, and mills like this one fed thousands of cargo holds. "The East Coast was once a breadbasket," Goff said. "This used to be the Silicon Valley of agriculture." But that breadbasket, after the advent of railroads, moved west, and so too did milling operations. No longer was a grist mill on every corner necessary to process the crops of the surrounding countryside.

And after people captured the power of fossil fuels, machines created volumes of power that tide mills couldn't touch. North of this site, the United Shoe Manufactory employed hundreds of people in the twentieth century. Tide power was feeble compared to the energy demands of so large an operation, and the factory used fossil fuel. Progress transformed the surrounding countryside into an urban landscape, and waterways like the Bass River silted in. Beverly's old corn mill was abandoned, the history uninspiring.

For the most part, structures like these fell in on themselves, and as the modern world evolved, development buried them. No longer useful in their intended function, mills needed new purpose if they were to be allowed to persist. We headed north, toward Annisquam and a tide mill Goff knew to be still standing as a residence. Little did we know this trip would be a twofer. As luck would have it, something caught Goff's eye as we crossed a bridge near Gloucester: a millstone standing upright against a riverside convenience store.

Millstones are often granite disks three feet in diameter, cut with radial grooves. They weren't good for much else beyond crushing grain, and they're incredibly heavy. So when one outlived its usefulness, it usually didn't go too far. When you find a millstone, there's a fair chance that there is or was a mill nearby.

The building propping up this millstone didn't betray many classic signs of a tide mill. It was a cobbled-together, addition-happy, barn-red convenience store. When one is looking for historic structures, window signs advertising cheap domestic beer are not exactly a screaming clue. But right there, on the side of the building, among all the glitzy advertising, was the dead giveaway: a sign that said Sawyer Old Mill. And if you looked through all the modern ephemera that had been added and stuck to the walls through the years, there was, indeed, the footprint of an old tide mill. An ebb tide roared through the narrow slough under the modern bridge, full of vigor, energy, potential.

Inside, Goff approached the pretty, twenty-something clerk at the counter, framed in a cluttered rectangle of lighters and energy pills. "We're researching tide mills, and we noticed this building. Do you have any information on the history of this building?" Goff asked of the young woman. She furrowed her brow, cocked her head to one side, as if he were speaking a foreign language. "You know, from the eighteenth century?"

Still wordless, she turned to look at the Indian owner counting money at the end of the counter. He looked up and paused for a second, likewise dumbfounded by the question and wordlessly shook his head. That ignorance was understandable, and the reason that a handful of tide mills existed like this: their identities changed as they were repurposed for the growing world around them. "Sorry," said the young woman, and without a second glance began to ring up the gentleman that had fallen in line behind us. It was a bummer that the history hadn't followed the mill, but we were lucky to have found another tide mill that had been hiding in plain sight all along.

A few miles up the road, we pulled into the driveway of what was once the William Hodgkins Tide Mill but was now a handsome and impeccably maintained residence. It had a stunning waterfront perch above the Annisquam River, where anchored sailboats bobbed softly, their bows pointed toward the outgoing tide. The exterior of the home had the boxy frame of the original mill and screamed of a long history, sturdiness, utility. A door to nowhere on the second floor was an opening where grain had once been pulleyed up to a loft. Although no one was home when we knocked, we figured the homeowner might not mind us looking around some in the yard, considering the property was for sale (for, as Goff and I later found out, $1.2 million).[85]

We descended a ramp to the home's boat dock, and there, under the house, in a stone-block lined sluice, were original posts and a few gears that had once turned as water rushed under them. That original hardware was still there because the sluice had been blocked shut. Before leaving, we peered in a window. The woodwork on the interior was exquisite, hardwood floors and patterned brick walls, massive, exposed beams supporting the walls and ceiling, worn smooth, bronzed deeply with the centuries.

Goff mused on what it might take to raise funds to buy the house and convert it to a tide mill museum. "There's just not enough interest," he said, "which is sad because these mills were the seeds of many communities. In many cases there was nothing there other than a few hardy farming families. Then come along these mills at water's edge, and things start to grow."

All of these tide mills, even the ones that have long since fallen into the muck, have stories, sometimes fantastic tales touched by historical celebrities. At Poplar Grove, for instance, an eighteenth-century estate in rural Mathews County, Virginia, stands the only remaining tide mill of perhaps dozens that once stood along the Chesapeake Bay and its tributaries. The mill dates to just after the Civil War. The aging weatherboards are on their last leg. Hurricane Isabel dislodged the mill's waterwheel in 2003. A local carpenter made a new wheel in 2015. As ever, the mill stands, a battered relic that's the very last of its kind.[86]

Sally Tompkins, possibly the only woman to be commissioned an officer in the Confederate Army, was born and raised at this estate. John Lennon bought Poplar Grove with his wife, Yoko Ono, just a few months before an obsessed and mentally ill fan murdered him outside his New York City apartment. Until her death in 2023, Poplar Grove's owner was an eccentric businesswoman who could be found driving a tractor around the sprawling estate well into her 80s, another in the series of the property's remarkable residents. Stories like these wash out to sea forever each time a mill tumbles into the tide.[87]

But most of all, these mills represent a time when Americans' lives were more directly tied to the natural rhythms of the Earth—the seasons and tides, the natural cycles that always offered the promise of new life. Goff would like to see at least a small portion of this heritage set up to educate future generations before that small connection to nature disappears forever.

One turn of fate that probably won't happen is using tidal energy once more to power our way to the future; the resource has its limitations. A handful of tidal energy stations exist around the world, producing power that's measured only in hundreds of megawatts, a tiny fraction of a percent of the world's annual energy needs. But there are undeniable facts: most of the energy on which we now rely, namely fossil fuel, is finite, and nonrenewable alternatives pose their own risks. Part of our legacy is harnessing the power of the Earth.[88]

There were a couple more tide mills I wanted to hit on my way south. One was in Quincy, Massachusetts, eight miles south of Boston. Sandwiched in between a CVS, a strip mall, and a car dealership, the Souther Tide Mill was faring remarkably well for being situated in an area decidedly lacking rustic New England charm.

Built in 1806, the grist mill burned in 1854 and was rebuilt soon afterward. A cadre of volunteers had done a lot of work to restore the mill to good historical shape, rebuilding an entire wall, and what's there now is a mishmash of original nineteenth century frames and walls and twenty-first century restorations (the inside is gutted), a reminder for those who care to look to Quincy's historical connection to the sea despite the concrete jungle that had been built right up to water's edge.[89]

But being that historical beacon opened Souther Tide Mill to other threats, too. The local homeless population found the sturdy walls a convenient place to wait out bitter Massachusetts winters. Preservationists had no option but to erect a chain-link fence to keep out interlopers, detracting from the historic vantage they were going for in the first place. And in a spot so far removed from a historic landscape, mustering enough commitment to keep a mill like Souther preserved, much less offering tours, has been challenging.

On my way to find one more off-the-beaten-path tide mill, I took the long way intentionally, and was rewarded for the effort. US Route 1, after an overland beeline straight from Boston to Providence, snakes along the craggy, southern New England coast. My gas gauge hit E nearing Warwick, Rhode Island, and inexplicably, there beside the service station, stood a familiar, boxy frame. Its mustard clapboard siding and large twelve-over-twelve sash windows had been lovingly tended through the years. "The Tide Mill Circa 1710," announced a long black-and-white sign. The old mill was now a design studio. After gassing up, I knocked on the door. No one home. But no matter. It gave me what I needed—hope and confirmation of what Goff had told me, that there are more undiscovered tide mills out there, being used as restaurants and homes and, as the case may be, design studios. Perhaps tide mills aren't as far gone as we suspected.

But there was one last mill I was eager to see to round out my whirlwind tour of this disappearing slice of American history, one that required an epic effort to attain and turned out to be only inches away from its last breath.

Though it may be hard to believe while mired in Long Island Expressway traffic, long ago, Long Island, New York, was a rural expanse, a patchwork of farms that never completely lost Dutch influences, even though the English had taken firm control in the second half of the seventeenth century. All those farms growing grain needed mills at every possible juncture. All the Dutch influences meant that windmills dotted the island and, of course, being surrounded by tidewater offered an additional means of milling all that grain.[90]

The late nineteenth century's opulence transformed large swaths of Long Island into gilded residences for the rich and famous. Later, suburban New York City spilled onto the former farmland the well-to-do hadn't claimed. The Long Island land grab left little nostalgia, not to mention need, for the mills that had transformed the tide's energy into usable power, and one by one, they vanished.[91]

That's why I wanted to see the last tide mill on Long Island—the Van Wyck-Lefferts Mill, a humble old mill that sits on Lloyd Harbor, one of the North Shore's stunningly picturesque havens laid thick with long lines of sailboats moored in the harbor.

My tour guide was Bob Rubner, a genial retiree and volunteer with the Huntington Historical Society. Rubner invited me to tag along with an already-scheduled tour of the mill. The good news was that the tour was overbooked—more than twenty people had signed up. Rubner had never seen so much interest in a mill that, though rare, had never really garnered such a level of attention. It was heartening.

The bad news was the same—the tour was overbooked, and getting to the physical site was already a challenge. Although the Nature Conservancy owned the mill and the dam on which it sat, the land all around it was a neighborhood whose residents weren't too keen on tour groups traipsing across their lawns to access a weathered old mill. And it might be one thing if this was some new neighborhood in an out-of-the-way corner of suburban America, but these homes were the inheritors of the gilded suburban New York City spillover. Their manicured yards sloped to the crystal water of Lloyd Harbor. There was a fat chance of overland access.

So we took a boat to get there. Actually, the skiff's captain made the ten-minute trip twice, dropping off the first load of passengers, then going back for the others since the boat couldn't hold everyone. And we had to tour the old mill within a precise window of time, since a too-low tide would have rendered the mill's mooring inaccessible by boat.

Outside, the boxy and weathered clapboard frame looked its two hundred-plus years old. Beside the noble old structure, a sturdy wooden tide gate that had once fit a now-free-flowing gap in the milldam sat rotting, chin-high weeds growing up around it. Inside the mill were the original gears and millstones, well-preserved. This is the hardware that had once turned, crushing grain that fed the largest city in the United States.[92]

But what struck me most about the Van Wyck-Lefferts mill was the level of the high tide, only inches beneath the short foundation. And this happened to be a normal tide. The first floor had been inundated many times, the most recent being during Hurricane Sandy. Even with a modest rise in sea level, it was apparent that, without drastic changes, this mill's days are numbered.

And that, conceded Rubner, was unlikely, given that preserving this part of history—never mind that this was the last of perhaps dozens on Long Island—was a low priority. We motored back to the dock, and I bid this this tide mill—and every other one—adieu. Staring out over the water of Lloyd Harbor, high dollar pleasure craft motored toward Long Island Sound. Cars zipped along the road that rimmed the opposite shore. Overhead, planes floated down into LaGuardia Airport. And at sea level, as tidewater slipped away, all that energy washed out to sea.

Chapter 5

The Garrett Farm: A Manhunt and a Median

The cavalrymen hustled into position around the old farmhouse. They were edgy, spent from the long chase, but the promise of financial reward tempered their exhaustion and drove them on. The soldiers' commander and two civilian detectives stormed the porch and dragged the pajamaed householder from his home into the cool April night. The officers threatened the old man, insisted he cooperate, all as his family looked on, but his garbled mumblings only drew anger. An interrogator drew a pistol, and the man's son could take no more. "The barn," he said. "The men you seek are in the barn."

Everyone within earshot looked to the shadowed form fifty yards off, realizing that just a few thin slats of siding were all that separated the manhunters from the most wanted person on Earth. Soldiers surrounded the darkened building, the officers barking orders to surrender. A voice boomed through the wall in response, playing dumb. "Who are you and what do you want?" A showman's voice. A guilty voice. The game was up, the stage set for John Wilkes Booth's last performance, a swan song as fiery and violent as a mad actor could produce.[93]

Flash forward a hundred and fifty years. You can stand in the spot where the most famous manhunt in United States history came to a bloody end, but you won't get a sense for much that went on that night. There are no ruins of any sort, and the lay of the land is no good for any historical perspective. You can listen all you want for voices dancing on the whispering wind, but they aren't there. This is, after all, a no man's land.

The wooded median of a rural four-lane highway is about as forgettable a landscape as they come. Grassy roadside fringe gives way to a tangle of brush and trees. People drive by these ribbons of foliage every day without a second thought. Stop and get out of your car and it feels cold, foreign, like you shouldn't be there. Long crescendos announce the screaming approach of eighteen-wheelers, which jostle everything as they whoosh by.

On one such stretch of US Route 301 in Caroline County, Virginia, a narrow gravel shoulder pulls off to the left side of the northbound lanes. Sometimes a simple sign points into the woods. Other times it's been removed by vandals or transportation crews, or just blown over by the wind. A narrow footpath slinks into the woods and ends up at a small clearing surrounded by an anemic forest.

You'd be hard-pressed to guess that anything at all happened on the spot, much less something of international renown. All that's there to mark this famous little patch of earth is a weathered iron rod sticking straight up, its end fluted from being sledged into the ground so hard. An official-looking sign promises potential relic hunters a stiff fine and a stint in the slammer.

A few steps from these humble monuments—if you can call them that—John Wilkes Booth gasped his last words and died, a dramatic end deserving some theatrical award, were it not real life. People come here from time to time to reflect on the significance of the first-ever United States presidential assassination, and the justice that his pursuers meted out on this very ground. All that sentimental retrospect is a little hard to muster, however, standing in a grove of scrubby trees with semis speeding by to rush squirt guns and T-shirts to the nearest big box store.

All this begs a simple question: What happened? After all, less noteworthy events have been afforded the honor of signage and statuary. No disrespect intended for our friends outside the Civil War's most-active theaters, but some of the "battles" commemorated in far-flung corners of the Union and Confederacy were, in reality, little more than trigger-happy home guards drinking a little too much booze and popping off a few Minié balls. And to be fair, the site of Booth's capture and death does, in fact, have an explanatory placard, although the weathered, thirty-four-word historical marker stands a few hundred yards from the actual site, on the other side of the road from where it all went down.

The eyes of not just the nation, but the world once focused on this little corner of Earth. It was the scene of a confrontation that outshone even four years of war, the porch where the flamboyant assassin John Wilkes Booth expired, the homestead where curious sightseers and looters came by the thousands to cart off mementos of this event. All of that happened on this littered median, passed unrecognized every minute by harried drivers eager to be any place but here.

A lot changed when Americans began putting bullets through one another in 1861, and the casualties went far beyond the human beings unlucky enough to be on the receiving end.

John Wilkes Booth shot President Lincoln probably anticipating a tidy aftermath. He'd make a quick getaway into Virginia and, from there, point south, all the while enjoying the comfortable shelter of well-heeled Confederates who'd toast his bravery for ridding the world of a despot. What he found instead was a plot that went off-script and concluded twelve days later a long way from where he thought he'd end up.

For one, Booth wasn't expecting a broken leg, but that's exactly what he got after putting a bullet point-blank into Lincoln's brain during a staging of *Our American Cousin* at Ford's Theatre in Washington, DC. That was the night of April 14, 1865, not yet a week after General Robert E. Lee's surrender at Appomattox. Ever the performer, Booth leaped from the president's box about eleven feet to the stage below, where he landed cockeyed and broke his fibula. The dashing actor nevertheless managed to hobble to mid-stage and take credit for the act. "Sic semper tyrannis," he shouted to the confused audience. "The South is avenged."[94]

The broken leg was an irksome turn of events, but not a show-stopper; Booth exited Ford's Theatre and rode off into the dark Maryland countryside before anyone really knew what was going on. There he met with Davey Herold, who had participated in the conspiracy by serving as a lookout while another accomplice attempted to murder Secretary of State William H. Seward. The bum leg meant Booth couldn't mount or dismount with ease, and the constant jostling of the horse's gait no doubt aggravated what was already excruciating pain. But Booth would be sure to find friends who would aid his escape. Or so he thought.

Yes, Booth and Herold came across sympathizers during their flight; many residents of southern Maryland and northeastern Virginia detested Lincoln and weren't crushed at news of his assassination. But even allies were nevertheless loath to shelter fugitives if being caught in the act meant certain imprisonment or worse. The aggrieved nation was lousy with threats of retribution for the president's killers. An official proclamation from the War Department five days after Lincoln's death said in no uncertain terms that anyone aiding assassination conspirators "shall be subjected to a trial before a Military Commission and the punishment of DEATH."[95]

Dr. Samuel Mudd's reaction was typical. He was a resident of Charles County, Maryland, who set Booth's broken leg and allowed the weary-looking pair a few hours' rest in his home. When Mudd discovered they were quite possibly involved in the president's death, he ordered them away at once but delivered them to neighbors sympathetic to their plight. Others offered what they could to help the fugitives to avoid detection, but opening their homes was out of the question. After Mudd evicted Booth and Herold, they spent nights in a pine thicket and boggy lowlands, not under a respectable roof, and traveled under the cover of darkness.[96]

Booth was crestfallen, indignant at his treatment. "After being hunted like a dog through swamps, woods and last night being chased by gun boats till I was forced to return wet cold and starving, with every man's hand against me, I am here in despair," wrote Booth after being refused shelter overnight at a farm called Indiantown in Maryland. "And why; For doing what Brutus was honored for, what made Tell a Hero."[97]

Booth simply gauged others' receptiveness wrong; he'd been a prosperous actor and city-slicker far removed from the rivers of blood that tainted the Confederate countryside. The families who left fathers and sons and neighbors on the battlefield, who saw war's cost firsthand, found the rhetoric hollow after four long years. For many Southerners, especially those directly affected by the Civil War, no amount of fiery zeal could reignite the itch they once had for a fight. That's why even ardent Confederate supporters gave Booth and Herold the cold shoulder. So when Booth found the type of hospitality he'd been expecting all along, the type of succor that dulled the pain of rejection, he tarried much too long for his own good—and ultimately visited ruin upon his unwitting hosts.

Locust Hill was the Caroline County, Virginia, farm of Richard H. Garrett, a prosperous farmer who had owned twenty-two enslaved people before the outbreak of war. When Booth and Herold showed up, Garrett was fifty-eight years old and lived at Locust Hill with a large family: his second wife, Fannie, and nine children ranging from three years old into their twenties.[98]

Garrett wasn't doing too bad for himself. By midcentury, he had amassed a spread of more than seven hundred acres. The Garretts and their enslaved laborers cultivated tobacco, corn, and wheat, and raised livestock. Still, Garrett, like every other Southerner, would have felt firsthand the effects of the war. His slaves were set free. The economy was in shambles. All things considered, though, the Garretts were lucky among Virginians. The farm never saw battle or bivouac. The two sons who went for Confederate service came back in one piece. They'd made it through a lot better than many of their fellow Southerners.[99]

That is, until Lincoln's assassin showed up.

Garrett and his children all insisted to their dying day they had no idea who they were harboring. Booth and Herold had a passable cover story. They went by pseudonyms. Booth was James William Boyd (matching perfectly the "J. W. B." tattoo on his forearm); Herold was David E. Boyd (who also had a more conspicuous "D. E. H." monogram tattoo which he had evidently tried to rub out). They were cousins, Marylanders, and Confederate veterans embittered by defeat and going south to continue the fight with hangers-on there. Booth explained away his leg injury as a wound sustained in the trenches at Petersburg.[100]

That yarn is what convinced Richard Garrett to take in "James William Boyd" when a trio of shifty ex-Confederate callers hastily deposited him there on their way south. Garrett said his religious convictions demanded he shelter the wounded man. Herold, or "David Boyd," continued south to Bowling Green, but promised to return soon.[101]

Locust Hill must have seemed like paradise to Booth. Sure, the six-room, two-story, white clapboard farmhouse wasn't the largest in the South, but for the first time in the ten days since he shot Lincoln, Booth faced the prospect of all the creature comforts he'd been denied since going on the lam.[102]

Booth ate a hearty supper with the Garretts, enjoyed a bowl of tobacco, and slept in a bedroom with the Garrett's adult sons Jack and Will and two younger children. So exhausted was Booth that he hit the sack and slept through breakfast the next morning. The following day Booth lay about in no particular hurry, reclining on Garrett's grass, playing with the kids. Booth was well-fed and relaxed. Herold returned that evening and the pair expected once more to be put up comfortably for the evening.

But something wasn't right, at least in the estimation of Jack and Will Garrett. Booth's invented backstory aside, the unexpected caller would have fit the widely circulated description to a T. The assassination was a heated topic of conversation at the church service Richard Garrett attended the day before Booth showed up. While the lame fugitive was at Locust Hill, Jack returned from a neighbor's telling of a $140,000 reward for the apprehension of Lincoln's killer. Booth, still in the role of Boyd, scoffed at that amount, saying it should be $500,000.

The strange behavior continued. Booth snapped at Jack Garrett, ordering him to retrieve his pistols when a handful of horsemen rode past the house. Later that day, after Herold returned to the Garrett farm, the dubious duo went off to hide in the woods as a squad of Federal cavalry flew past—soldiers who would return to the Garrett place several hours later.

It was all a bit too hinky, so Jack Garrett refused to let the men sleep in the farmhouse. Instead, their bedroom for the evening was the tobacco barn, an imposing outbuilding near the house. Even with the shady visitors now outside their home, Jack and Will Garrett took no chances, thinking them scoundrels who'd steal their horses in the dark of night. The Garretts locked the Boyds inside the barn and slept in the nearby corncrib just in case.[103]

And for several hours, it seemed that there'd be no more mischief at Locust Hill. At about two in the morning, though, that all changed. The dogs began barking, the air filled with the clanging of military accoutrements. The same detachment that had dashed past

Locust Hill earlier had returned with good intelligence on the whereabouts of Booth and Herold. Cavalrymen encircled the farmhouse. When it became clear their quarry was in the barn, the soldiers surrounded it and ordered Booth and Herold out. Herold surrendered when he realized the manhunt was over, but Booth would not be taken so easily.

"Give a lame man a chance," Booth said through the barn wall in the squabbling that ensued. He challenged the squad to a ridiculous twenty-seven-against-one gunfight.

No, Detective Luther Baker told him in reply, we've come to take you prisoner, not to fight.

Booth couldn't let go of a spectacular end. He fancied himself a gamecock, a man who claimed he had too great a soul to die like a criminal. "Withdraw your forces a hundred yards from the door, and I will come out," pleaded Booth. "Give me a chance for my life, Captain, for I will not be taken alive."

The officers were in no mood for bargaining, or for theatrics, so Detective Everton Conger lit some kindling that had been piled against an outside wall of the barn. The idea was that the flames would force Booth out of the barn where he could be taken alive and whisked back to Washington, DC, for trial.[104]

Cue the plot twist. One of the cavalrymen positioned around the barn was a sergeant named Boston Corbett who had a carbine and such a loose grip on sanity he had cut off his own balls before the war. Peering through the spaced slats, and by his own admission directed by God, Corbett shot Booth. The bullet struck Booth behind his ear and severed his spine, exiting out a front quarter of his neck. Immediately he fell to the floor, paralyzed by the injury, stunned by the sucker punch.[105]

Soldiers carried Booth first to a patch of earth under some nearby locust trees. He tried to utter a few last words but was too weak. "Tell mother . . . tell mother," was all he could manage. Finally, he whispered what many supposed would be his last words: "Tell mother I died for my country." But it turns out that phrase was a bit premature.[106]

When the heat of the blazing barn became too intense, those gathered around Booth moved him to the porch of the farmhouse.

Lucinda Holloway, Richard Garrett's sister-in-law, provided what little relief she could. She brought Booth a straw mattress and laid his limp body on it. She dipped a handkerchief into water and moistened the dying man's lips. They offered him wine, but he refused. They sent for a doctor.

All the while, the gaping wound hemorrhaged, Booth's blood staining the planks of the porch beneath him. Booth couldn't get comfortable, and he requested to be moved this way and that, unable to make those adjustments himself. When the town doctor arrived, he pronounced Booth's condition hopeless. All present except Booth, who'd already made plain his desire to die, would've preferred the assassin to explain himself in court, to face the aggrieved nation. But the wound was mortal. One of the attendants held up Booth's hands and the actor uttered his final line: "Useless, useless."[107]

Those last words dripped with so much meaning, so many interpretations. Yes, his hands were functionally useless, but was he commenting on something larger? Lincoln's assassination? The Confederate cause? Booth's meaning went to the grave with him.

At that moment there would have been another conspicuous player in this drama harboring a sense of futility: Richard Garrett. The smoldering ruins of what had been his tobacco barn presented a bad omen for Locust Hill. Those charred timbers represented decades of hard work. All the implements the Garretts needed to get by in what were certain to be tough years ahead went up in smoke.

The barn itself was no flimsy structure, forty-eight by fifty feet, anchored by heavy cedar posts and joists, a plank floor throughout, designed for hanging and curing Virginia gold. The list of tools Garrett kept in that barn reads like some nineteenth century farmer's catalog: a wheat thrashing machine and mill, scythes, plows, a harrow, barrels, not to mention hundreds of pounds of animal feed. Garrett had also volunteered the space for storage of valuables from townsfolk whose homes were on the Rappahannock River and therefore vulnerable to shelling by Federal gunboats. Alongside all the agricultural hardware were tables, chairs, beds, a chest, and shoemaker's tools. The value of all that burned that night came in at more than $2,600—no small blow considering a private in the Union Army earned just sixteen dollars a month.

Garrett didn't receive a dime in compensation. He petitioned the United States government to reimburse him, insisting all along he had no idea of Booth's true identity until the assassin lay dying on his farm—a claim a congressional committee on war claims found far-fetched. "He had abundant opportunity to learn, and sufficient circumstances existed from which he might infer who Booth was," mused the report, calling Garrett "undoubtedly disloyal." No matter, though. Garrett's loyalty was irrelevant. Citing a long list of precedents, the report found the tobacco barn "was destroyed in regular military operations at a time when war was flagrant in Virginia." Garrett was entitled to nothing.[108]

That stung and sent Locust Hill into a death spiral. True, Garrett still had a roof over his head and land to farm, but his net worth was a fraction of what it once was. In 1860, the value of his personal property was $16,000. Ten years later, that was $600. The twenty-two slaves emancipated accounted for much of that loss. The tobacco barn compounded the farm's economic troubles. Garrett nevertheless had little time to sulk; neighbors swore that Garrett was a man of modest means and that his large family depended on the fruits of his labor. There was work to be done.[109]

In hindsight, Garrett might have improved his circumstances had he milked his fifteen minutes of fame a little more. Others certainly did. The public's appetite for all things Lincoln-assassination was insatiable from day one. Play-by-play accounts of the shooting and manhunt were front page news. Rumor and speculation were rampant: "History has on its record no suicidal act so terrible as that committed by the conquered South yesterday through its representative, the assassin of President Lincoln," reported Washington's *Evening Star* the day after Lincoln's shooting.[110]

Among the most immediate topics of conversation were Booth's whereabouts. The same edition of the paper that fingered the South inaccurately reported Booth's arrest fifteen miles west of Baltimore but conceded that news might be premature. Booth-spotting wasn't restricted to Greater Washington, DC. There were false sightings all over. In Great Mills, Maryland, Booth was seen dressed as a woman.

Booth fever even reached across the Atlantic. "There was a good deal of excitement yesterday in Queenstown [now Cobh, Ireland] when, on the arrival of the passengers from the Inman steamer Edinburgh, it was whispered that John Wilkes Booth, the reputed assassin of President Lincoln, had been arrested and brought ashore," reported the *Liverpool Mercury* in early May 1865 (after a little rough treatment, the poor look-alike was set free).[111]

Booth's capture did little to quell intense public interest in the conspiracy. According to Lucinda Holloway, Garrett's sister-in-law, the ramshackle porch became a shrine; thousands of people stopped by the Garrett place to lay eyes on the exact spot where Booth expired. Even before Locust Hill became a macabre tourist attraction, Holloway sensed correctly that relics associated with the assassination were going to be a hot commodity. She claimed to have asked the attending doctor to clip a lock of Booth's hair after he died and sought to send to her mother's house a pair of opera glasses Booth left behind. A Union Army officer later came by to retrieve them.[112]

There was reward money for the soldiers and detectives who captured Booth. Despite his handsome payout (each man present got more than $1,600) there's one relic Private Frederick Deitz wished years later he had thought to pick up. Like Boston Corbett, Deitz was one of the cavalrymen positioned around the doomed barn. Deitz remembered the instant Corbett fired. "The ball went clear through Booth's neck, through the back part of the barn, and dropped within a pace of me. I could see it knock up the dirt. I never thought to pick it up. If I had, I might have made a fortune out of it."[113]

The mad grab for assassination artifacts included the farmhouse's porch. Holloway claimed someone made a substantial offer for the wood plank stained by Booth's blood. No telling if Garrett made good on that particular deal, but pieces of the porch, or reputed pieces of the porch anyway, eventually found themselves into the hands of collectors.[114]

In 1902, the National Herb Company in Washington, DC, advertised a display of what the firm claimed was the best specimen of Garrett porch wood. "The boards upon which the assassin breathed his last were removed at the time, and for years small pieces were sold to sight seers [*sic*]. The largest one (size 6 × 13 ¼ inches) ever taken from the premises can be seen at our offices."[115]

There were even plans to dismantle, ship, reconstruct, and display the Garrett house at the Chicago World's Fair, but that scheme, for whatever reason, never came together. P. T. Barnum, of circus fame, made an offer to buy a saddle Booth briefly occupied during his flight from justice. Even co-conspirators wanted to make a buck off the ordeal. Thomas Jones aided Booth's escape by hiding him and Herold in a pine thicket for five days and four nights, bringing them food and furnishing a rowboat. In the years afterward, Jones was a dealer of assassination relics.[116]

The assassination craze meant little for the Garretts and Locust Hill, though. For his part, Richard Garrett seems to have just wanted the whole thing to disappear, so he could go about his business. When Holloway asked him what to do with those opera glasses that Booth left behind, he ordered them out of his sight. "I do not want to see anything that will remind me of the dreadful affair," he said.

But getting on with things was easier said than done. Approaching sixty years old, Garrett was past his prime. And if his sister-in-law is to be believed, he fell ill the night his barn burned and never really recovered. Twice Holloway mentioned that the roughhousing by Federals made the old man sick.[117]

So Garrett was infirm and elderly, with other mouths to feed, far removed from the prewar prosperity he had once enjoyed. And if those weren't obstacles enough to resuming normalcy, the Garretts also found few friends willing to help them out in an era rife with finger-pointing and grudges.

When Jack and Will Garrett were taken to an arsenal for questioning about any possible role in the assassination, a lynch mob gathered outside, wanting their heads. The unruly crowd dispersed at the sight of more armed guards and big guns. Many in the mourning nation thought that the Garretts were complicit in the assassination—that they were, in effect, conspirators who got off. And Southerners who resented the postwar occupation by Federal troops thought the Garretts somehow had a hand in helping the detested Yankees who now occupied their land.[118]

So harsh and wide was the criticism leveled against the Garretts that Richard Garrett's son, named Richard Baynham Garrett, embarked on a multi-state speaking tour in the 1890s to clear his family's name. "Standing beside the dead body my father heard for the first time that the man who for two days had been his guest was the man who had killed the President," he told audiences.

Old Richard Garrett never returned to the comfortable life he'd known before the Civil War, and he died in 1878 (an end Holloway called "premature," but there's no telling if he'd have lived longer without being roughed up that night; he was seventy-two years old, past the life expectancy of the day). Garrett's second wife Fannie followed him to the grave two and a half years later. Locust Hill never returned to its prewar robustness either. The Garretts rebuilt the barn, but their efforts were no match for all that conspired against them. Family members, wishing to distance themselves from the stigma brought on by their unsolicited callers, eventually abandoned their old home to make families and farms of their own elsewhere.

"My father's sin was in giving shelter to a wounded suffering soldier, and what Virginian would not have committed that sin? Yet he the aged Christian man, for this sin (?) was financially ruined and his last days shortened and embittered by cruel and unjust charges," wrote Richard B. Garrett in 1882. "A lonely grave, a desolate and decaying homestead, a scattered family, bear mute testimony to the wrong done us not only by the Government, but by our friends."[119]

The abandoned house became a victim to the forces of nature and relic hunters who raided the old ruins. Without proper attention, decay set in. The metal roof rusted clean through, letting rain fall on the interior. The pine weatherboard rotted and fell off a few long planks at a time. The brick chimneys at either end of the house collapsed. Looters removed anything they could salvage or sell from the ruins of the historic home. "All the mantels have been taken away and some of the doors and windows have been removed," wrote a worker from Virginia's Works Progress Administration Historical Inventory Project after she visited the house in 1937. "It seems on the verge of collapsing."[120]

And collapse it did, not too long after that. A few years later, as the United States' involvement in World War II became more certain, the government acquired more than seventy-five thousand acres for large-scale military training—a facility that would eventually become Fort Walker. What had been Locust Hill was now government property, off limits, and with live-fire and maneuverability training going on around it, generally not a good place to be snooping about. Natural growth—pines, hardwoods, and locusts that gave the farm its name—shrouded the traces of the old Garrett place, erasing the structures where Booth enjoyed short-lived southern hospitality. A *Washington Post* reporter visited the site of the Garrett House in 1951. He found only rotten beams and broken bricks—a heap of rubble choked with briars. Presumably, the rebuilt tobacco barn, along with all the other outbuildings at Locust Hill, shared the same fate.[121]

Even though people once flocked to Locust Hill for curiosity's sake, or to take relics, no one ever spoke much about preserving this site for posterity, or if they did, no movement ever picked up steam. Perhaps the site just had too many uncomfortable associations. Or maybe folks wanted to avoid the trouble that visited the Garretts. And even if preservation efforts had somehow gained traction, the old Garrett place was only ruins, and off-limits ruins at that. Society left Locust Hill to its own demise.

But even that doesn't explain how that old farmhouse where Booth expired took that extra step from ruin to its permanent, purgatorial state in a wooded median. As it turns out, the very same trait that brought the Garrett place fame also secured its place in that perennial no man's land.

The real Confederate soldiers Booth latched onto toward the end of his flight gladly rid themselves of him at Locust Hill in large part because it was convenient—right on the road between Port Royal and Bowling Green, the route they happened to be taking. Years later, about the time the WPA worker was visiting that pitiable shell of the Garrett house, other Depression-era workers paved that road. Three decades later, planners deemed those two paved lanes insufficient, so they added two more lanes north of the existing highway. Bulldozers graded a right-of-way, laid a bed, and paved a road through the spot where the manhunt for John Wilkes Booth came to an end.[122]

Although the median and the iron pipe marking the spot where the Garretts' west chimney once stood are officially off limits, "curiosity lovers and seekers," as Holloway called them, still call on the old homestead to stand on this ground. There's not much to see, and if you're looking to get a sense for the drama that unfolded here, the din of traffic won't help you. That Locust Hill has now vanished from the map says as much about the arc of American history as the events that unfolded here in April 1865.

CHAPTER 6

Mallows Bay: Nature Claims a Boondoggle

Americans love a good monument. Just ask the nice folks of Enterprise, Alabama, who pay homage to the boll weevil, a pest that laid waste to local cotton crops of the nineteen-teens, forcing farmers to diversify what they produced. Or chat with the fine citizens of Lincoln, Illinois, who rally behind their mascot, a watermelon sculpture, because way back in 1853, Honest Abe Lincoln, the town's namesake and future president, poured the juice from that humble fruit on the ground, christening the land.

One August morning, my friend John Gulick and I made for a public boat ramp deep in Charles County, Maryland. John is a science teacher, and I brought him along because the national monument we'd be visiting was, in fact, no monument at all—no imposing phallus, nor some nude-bedecked Greco-Roman temple. No, this was more an unintended tribute to madness, a collective effort forgotten just as quickly as it occurred. I wanted a scientific perspective on what had happened in the long interim since.

Though only thirty miles south of the nation's capital, the eastern bank of the Potomac River in Charles County, Maryland, is a world away. Getting to Mallows Bay from just about anywhere, John and I discovered, is not a straight shot. The roads are narrow and winding, and the route begins to seem interminable as it snakes through forest that's old and lush. John and I had long since exhausted our topics of conversation when he decided to break the silence.

"This would be a really good place to hide a body," he said, gazing out the window at the swaths of dense and uninterrupted forestland. His deadpan comment came out of nowhere and would have been a bit unnerving except for the fact that his reflection was oddly apropos. We would, indeed, be seeing concealed corpses of a sort, and I told him as much.

A few minutes after John's observation, we arrived at a public boat landing that looked new and, by all indications, gently used. A well-graded gravel parking lot and a smooth asphalt road curved down a steep slope to a single boat ramp. The place lacked the detritus of the Potomac River's more popular urban access points: scattered beer cans and tangled monofilament, the remnants of what may or may not have been successful fishing. Though well-tended, the landing betrayed the signs of an eventful history that had faded from memory. To one side of the ramp was some abandoned lagoon, hemmed in by a cofferdam of cracked concrete and corrugated steel, trying for all the world to return to a natural state.

We slipped our kayaks into the flat water, and the ripples lapped our hulls. A couple light paddle strokes opened the distance between land and shore. We pointed our bows straight ahead because that seemed as good a place as any to begin this exploratory voyage. Dead center was a massive, weather-beaten steel hulk, rusted deep copper, looking as though the captain pointed her east, ran her hard aground, and swam off, never to return. But I knew that the old behemoth was merely a distraction and ordered a change of course.

"Over here," I said, turning north toward a line of pilings pocked and green with age.

"A shipwreck? Isn't that what we came here for?" John asked.

"Yes, but not that one. That's an old car ferry," I explained, gesturing toward the rusted shell. "That boat came a lot later. The ones we want are this way."

John shrugged and nosed his bow north, too, seeming incredulous there was wreckage as worthy of exploration as the huge carcass we were turning away from. Once we had paddled past the pilings, though, the skeletons began to appear.

"What are those things? Turtles?" John asked of a row of knobs now silhouetted against the glare of the water's glossy surface. Indeed, the line of sharp stubs we approached looked very much like when you see a distant speck above the surface and can't tell whether it's a turtle or a stick or something else entirely. Only there were hundreds of these shadowy points. Thousands, even. And they were aligned in an odd geometrical pattern that was hard to make sense of from sea level. What's more, among all these old bones were several incongruous landforms teeming with life, verdant islands amid a sea of wreckage. We had come upon the first of 170-odd sunken wrecks crammed into this shallow cove off the Potomac River. The scale of the junkyard was formidable, impressive and, in a way, heartbreaking. All that effort for this. All that effort for nothing.

"Here it is," I told John. "This is what's left of the World War I emergency fleet of wooden steamships."

I paddled over one of the submerged hulls and stepped out of the kayak into twelve inches of water. I was standing on the wooden deck of a ship that last floated many decades ago. The hull was not watertight but remained intact thanks to a frame of crisscrossed iron strapping—the top of which made the stubs we'd seen from afar.

I launched into the history I'd read of the Mallows Bay derelicts before venturing here, but John—more interested in the here-and-now than the long ago—paddled off to float by a nearby osprey nest. I stood on that foredeck in awe, admiring the craftsmanship that was still evident in these old boats, happy to be standing on so impressive a collection of shipwrecks. I realized that the odd giddiness I felt just then in some ways mimicked the excited frenzy that had led to the creation of this fleet long ago.

The whole idea was that the United States, brimming with patriotic fervor by 1916, was going to build ships faster than German U-boats could sink them. In a rare example of understatement, policymakers called the threat "the submarine menace." But there wasn't enough steel for such an ambitious fleet, so the United States Shipping Board opted for what they deemed the next best thing and ordered hundreds of wooden steamships—workaday merchant vessels that would supply foreign ports with all the supplies necessary to keep fighting men functioning "Over There." Turns out all that flag-waving was no match for the daunting practical realities of such an undertaking. Still, the US, confident from the spanking it had delivered Spain nearly two decades before, not to mention President Teddy Roosevelt's peacockery with the Great White Fleet, was willing to give it a shot, logistic issues be damned.[123]

Far away from Mallows Bay in coastal New England, the swift Piscataqua River opens up for its last six miles to form Portsmouth Harbor—an ideal spot, thought the owners of L.H. Shattuck Shipyard, for building the eighteen wooden steamship hulls the US government ordered from them. The fact that Shattuck's 110-acre site just north of Portsmouth, in Newington, wasn't the least bit ready for such an endeavor concerned the yard owners little. Practically, however, that meant crews had to clear land and construct shipways—a years-long process—in order to lay the first keel.[124]

The story was the same all over the United States, shipyards appearing out of thin air, as the June 1917 issue of *International Marine Engineering* described: "One shipyard on Puget Sound is turning out ships to-day [*sic*] on a piece of waterfront which fifteen months ago was nothing more than a meeting place for land and tide." All told, the Shipping Board placed orders for 731 ships at ninety-three shipyards scattered around the country, many of which were like those at Portsmouth and Puget Sound—scarcely ready to assemble ocean-going vessels.[125]

Jury-rigged shipyards weren't the only problem that plagued the wooden shipbuilding program. So too did the rich claims made by the effort's early cheerleaders: the United States could produce a thousand wooden ships in sixteen months. A single ship would take only four months. Perhaps a cocksure nation buoyed by patriotic fervor couldn't see what a laughably tall order that was.[126]

And then there were problems of supply: wood capable of making a seaworthy ship, laborers experienced enough to make that possible. Elmer Brooks, a worker at Shattuck Shipyard, recalled in an interview with *Yankee* magazine in 1970 that the men who worked through the long hours and cramped, grueling conditions with him there were "butchers and barbers . . . woodchoppers, farm boys, beer drinkers," men who came from "down Maine, way up in New Hampshire where they never see a mailman." While all these good old boys might have been salt-of-the-earth Americans who would be a hoot to bring to the family barbecue, they were hardly the type of experienced craftsmen able to turn out high quality merchant vessels in no time flat. That the government offered bonuses, a whopping two hundred dollars a day, for vessels delivered ahead of schedule was even more reason for shipyards to approach their commissions with something less than due diligence.[127]

Shattuck didn't launch its first ship, the *Roy H. Beattie*, until July 4, 1918, four months before World War I ended. In fact, all the nation's shipyards had delivered only ninety-seven wooden vessels by war's end, a mere seventy-two of which had delivered cargo. A handful of these merchant vessels delivered coastwise goods, but none had made transatlantic voyages to the war zone—the reason they were commissioned in the first place. So much for the thousand-ship fleet.[128]

When word of an armistice came, crews at Shattuck had already begun work on a ship named *Dover*. Like more than two hundred other vessels already in some stage of production, the Shipping Board allowed Shattuck to finish it, but the inauspiciously named Division of Cancellation, Adjustment and Salvage voided 450 contracts. Letting workers build out what they'd begun was just a courtesy to the laborers giving so much to this effort and the ships that seemed like a good idea at the outset of the mission. There was a glaring problem, though: even as the *Dover* slid off its shipway into Portsmouth Harbor in 1919, long after hostilities had ended, its purpose had long since passed. Indeed, all these vessels were stillborn when seawater first touched their planks, because in an age of oil-burning, steel-hulled vessels, a wooden steamer was a dinosaur.[129]

Men who served aboard the wooden steamships had few kind words for them, and that, as much as anything, was their death knell. James L. Bonnett, who served aboard the *Coweta* in 1918, called it the "clumsiest, contrariest, awkwardest vessel I ever sailed on." It was caked in coal soot and prone to come apart in rough seas. On one occasion, its rudder simply fell off within sight of land in the Gulf of Mexico. About the only kind words that Bonnet could muster on wooden ships was that "they did the job, but little more," and that sunken ones made for good fishing.[130]

After realizing what dead weight it had on hand, the US government dolled up ads to try to sell its wooden fleet, including unfinished ships. The ships "should be attractive in view of the present prices for completed vessels," claimed a November 1919 advertisement in the *Nautical Gazette*.[131]

There were some takers, too, and that's how the *Dover* escaped the same end as a couple hundred other ships just like it. The Davison Chemical Company of Baltimore bought the *Dover* and two other vessels to use as barges for hauling pyrite ore between Cuba and its Baltimore plant, where it was processed for any copper they could coax out of it. Fifteen more wooden hulls became a breakwater just off the shores of Baltimore's Curtis Bay.[132]

All told, the government moved fifty-six wooden ships, but was forced to sell the rest, 227 of them, at a jaw-dropping loss, three-quarters of a million dollars for the lot, the price originally paid for one ship. Critics of the shipbuilding program gratuitously heaped scorn on the whole affair. "The war's greatest shipping blunder," postwar Shipping Board Chairman Albert Lasker called it. "A monument to folly."[133]

A firm out of Alexandria, Virginia, called Western Marine and Salvage Company, Inc. (WM&SC) bought the ships intending to scrap the metal on board (the wood was worthless) and netted in the neighborhood of $6,700 per ship—a handsome profit given that they'd acquired each ship for roughly half that. The bits barely held down, such as chains and boilers, were easy pickings, but the iron pegs and strapping that held the hulls together were a lot trickier. In fact, so hard to get was this hardware that WM&SC devised a ludicrously cumbersome scheme for retrieving it: they'd burn each hull to the waterline, haul the charred carcass ashore by a marine railway, and incinerate the rest of the wood, leaving nothing but metal.[134]

It's no wonder why locals at Widewater, Virginia, where WM&SC first tried this scheme, fumed about this. Smoke and ash poisoned the air and water, driving off fish that local watermen counted on for their livelihood. Instead of fighting this mom-and-pop opposition, the company simply moved their fleet of derelict ships two and a half miles east across the Potomac to Mallows Bay. But the shipbreaking proved no more successful there, and in 1932 WM&SC went belly up, claiming a $255,000 loss. The ships no longer offered easy profit, so WM&SC turned their backs to them, leaving a shallow cove on the eastern bank of the Potomac cluttered with nearly two hundred ships that no one wanted.[135]

Then a funny thing happened. Japan, ambitious but lacking in natural resources, decided to terrorize its neighbors. The price of scrap metal went from two dollars to twenty dollars a ton, and those rotting, half-sunken ships in Mallows Bay all of a sudden took on a new charm.[136]

The derelicts in Mallows Bay lit up once again, this time with hundreds of independent salvors—"idle farmers and fishermen" one witness called them—combing over the wrecks daily, selling scrap to middlemen who, in turn, sold to dealers in distant cities. This was, after all, the Great Depression, and starving laborers looked to make a buck wherever they could find it.[137]

"About 20 small boats here are loading scrap iron being removed from the burned wooden ships ashore," recorded fifteen-year-old Robert Fountain Hedges Jr., a Sea Scout (a nautical version of internationally popular scouting organizations), on July 26, 1931, after witnessing the spectacle at Mallows Bay. One scrap dealer unsuccessfully sued to have all the abandoned boats littering Mallows Bay deemed his. A report claimed there were twenty-six liquor stills aboard the wrecks. And relieved of heavy metal bracing by the freelance salvagers, a few hulks regained buoyancy and floated toward the busy shipping channel. The scene was, by many accounts, a wild, unregulated free-for-all.[138]

During World War II, the Bethlehem Steel Corporation launched another commercial effort to liberate the estimated twenty thousand tons of metal aboard the wooden vessels in Mallows Bay. They cordoned off a lagoon and built a cofferdam (the one at the foot of the modern-day boat ramp), all in an effort to reignite another version of WM&SC's failed scheme to burn the fleet into submission. That, too, ended in failure when the sticky, black mud from the floor of the Potomac oozed over the ships, extinguishing the flames and all hope that the derelict vessels would surrender their elusive iron skeletons.[139]

There'd be no more serious efforts to move the hulks, but still many locals were loath to accept the wrecks they deemed an eyesore, a demonstrable hazard to navigation. A few folks demanded the US government take care of them. One Maryland congressman tried to convince the feds to order them removed. He said that removing the wrecks could put impoverished people to work. A state legislator wooed the Navy, suggesting the hulks would make good practice for demolition teams. None of those ideas ever floated, though, and the ships languished in Mallows Bay, where they remain to this day.[140]

In 1962, the wrecks claimed the life of a father of four. For whatever reason, he loaded his kids on a small boat and nudged it into Mallows Bay to investigate something he saw bobbing in the water. Who knows what he thought the object was? What he found was a submerged vessel, or a big chunk of one anyway, that had somehow regained buoyancy. The man's craft capsized, and while he managed to heave his children back into the stricken boat, he was not so lucky himself.[141]

More than five decades after that regrettable mishap, John and I likewise found out that the hulks littering Mallows Bay are not to be approached recklessly; the same sharp hardware that frustrated decades of salvors lurks at the waterline, and often just below. After fifteen minutes of exploring, we'd drifted apart, but John found something he wanted me to see and beckoned me with a whistle. Getting there was not a straight shot. More than once my kayak scraped against rusty iron strapping, and I winced as the hull of my relatively feeble craft snagged on the steamships' jagged frames, gouging a thin curlicue of plastic. I learned to look a few boat lengths ahead just below the surface for these underwater hazards. Often, I successfully navigated the sharp metal only to run hard upon the ships' wooden planks requiring the humiliating hip-and-torso thrusts to earn release.

At last I made it to John, who was paddling around an island that was not-so-curiously shaped exactly like a boat's hull. A long line of iron pegs stood motionless, their heads six inches above the surface. Judging by their numbers, they had once held fast some integral part of the ship. Water swirled languidly around them. Beyond those pegs, timbers sat high enough above the water to support a wilderness in miniature.

"Look at all the diversity," John said. "There are aquatic and terrestrial plants. Grasses, shrubs, and trees. It's quite a mix. And that's just the vegetation." Up close, the thicket fluttered with the movement of insects, some impulsive and wary, others graceful and oblivious. Flowers bloomed en masse. What had been from afar an anomaly on the water's surface was, up close, a teeming community.

"What you don't see are all the dozens of species that are hidden in there or that come in for a quick meal and leave," John explained. As if on cue, a titmouse dropped in on a branch, causing it to sway like a one-sided seesaw. "You've got an entire food chain, a self-contained ecosystem right here. This is probably what large parts of islands and shorelines would look like if there were no humans."

John said he wasn't sure what sort of life he'd expected to find around shipwrecks, but having some of them exposed above water was a pleasant surprise. "These have gone through a long succession and have now settled into a sort of balance, and it's all because of this." He floated over and rubbed a pinky along a rotten timber at the edge of the island. The ships' wood had given the seeds the organic base they needed to take off.

The ships in Mallows Bay command respect for being all at once dangerous and beautiful, historic and alive. And that's to say nothing of the admiration they warrant for the improbability of their being here.

These ruined wrecks began life as works of craftsmanship—not the type of exquisite design of museum quality, but the homespun, folk-art sort. A quarter of a million Americans, from engineers to lumbermen to common laborers, roughnecks with little experience who came out of the woods for a common cause, managed to pull the whole thing off. Sure, the wooden shipbuilding program was flawed at almost every turn, but the country asked for hundreds of wooden ships and got them.

There's no helping that the wooden steamers were victims of circumstance. That wasn't their fault or the fault of the men who made them. Lucky for those ships, for all who care to notice them, something changed.

The derelict fleet in Mallows Bay, once scorned, took on value for what it became when nature took over. A 1966 *Washington Post* photo caption characterized them as "overgrown with seaweed and trees . . . half-hidden in the Potomac," and a congressional committee in 1970 called them "strange islands" that were "not at all unattractive," thanks in large part to the plants and animals that had long since taken up residence there. In fact, Congress ultimately refused any further federal action on the derelicts precisely because nature had colonized them so thoroughly.[142]

Now, they offer sanctuary to creatures for whom habitat would otherwise be hard to come by. And it didn't take wildlife long to find these hulks. Robert Hedges, the Sea Scout who saw so many salvors working the wrecks at Mallows Bay in 1931, also made note of the prodigious animals there: "Thousands of snowy white egrets nest in these old hulks," he wrote.[143]

The ships littering Mallows Bay reflect not only an odd wartime episode but also the Chesapeake Bay's fortunes. The water that once blanketed this mothballed fleet was among the most polluted in the country, a blemish on the national capital just upstream. But ever since humans have made efforts to stop mistreating the environment, species that took the biggest hit because of it—bald eagles and striped bass, for instance—have since bounced back in a big way and populate the wrecks that found little love. The ships are recognized as a heron rookery and a site where striped bass spawn.[144]

Mallows Bay today is a study in contrasts: the jagged metal bracing of the decayed hulks sloshed by the soft waves of the Potomac; the wooded shoreline, silent and still, a far cry from the industrial shipbreaking works there almost a century ago; most telling of all, the ships themselves, once scorned by the very people who made them, now prized for the sanctuary they have become.

Chapter 7

Watts Island: The Wet Fate of a Chesapeake Hermitage

Charles Hardenberg needed to get away. He had just finished an arduous and heartbreaking obligation: providing end-of-life care for his father. "I had to spend hours and days with him," he said of the ordeal years later. "I had a lot of time to think. When it was all over, I was tired; tired of everything, of the way we live and of the cities." It was 1908, and Hardenberg—a thirty-two-year-old Princeton-educated lawyer—took stock of his life. He was overworked and unhappy. Something had to change. A friend bet Hardenberg he couldn't separate himself from society for a decade. Incredibly, Hardenberg was willing to give it a shot.

Hardenberg soon surrendered civilization for a couple sandy specks of land way out in the Chesapeake Bay. Watts Island, at about three hundred acres, and Little Watts Island, less than three, had a combined population of exactly one. A keeper tended the lighthouse on Little Watts, separated from its uninhabited bigger sibling by several hundred yards of water. An old, abandoned farmhouse stood on Watts, just north of Little Watts, and Hardenberg moved in there. Within a few years, however, even the lighthouse keeper left, and Hardenberg became the only human being for at least five miles in every direction. There he stayed for the better part of three decades—alone, away, content.[145]

Like countless islanders before him, Hardenberg was spellbound by the mystique of living on a remote patch of land. Islands have long been immortalized in legend and literature. There is risk that goes along with living on an isolated speck, but that hasn't stopped people from trying to tame them, especially in the Chesapeake Bay, the bosom of modern American civilization.

There are hundreds of islands in the bay and its tributaries, and humans have left a footprint on nearly all of them. Some of the traces people left behind are quirky and extraordinary, hatching harebrained schemes to strike it rich, and constructing hermitages where recluses lived out their days free from prying eyes. Most efforts at island life were far more mundane, organic communities that grew from their proximity to the water, small collections of the humble dwellings of farmers and fishermen.

No matter their history or motivations, islanders all had one thing in common: they always kept a wary eye on the sea. They winced when waves carried off a small part of the ground beneath them. Nature has a way of emphasizing that humans' residences are temporary, that the dry ground they inhabit will one day exist no more.

Hardenberg discovered this truth, and it tore at him. He vowed to live on his island kingdom until his last breath, but he watched the waves batter the shoreline, the tides get a little higher each day and he realized the Chesapeake Bay had other plans. This is the story of two tiny islands in the Chesapeake Bay, but in truth, it's the story of all of them, an endless cycle of birth, death, love, and loss.

Watts and Little Watts were a long way from the gritty streets of Jersey City in 1908, a city of coal smoke and industrial clanging, a harried city that never slept. No telling if Hardenberg knew when he arrived in the bay that the wide expanse of water around him was the flooded valley of the ancient Susquehanna River; that the sea level had been rising for the past twenty thousand years; that the islands he'd now call home were once blunt ridges that towered over a broad ravine carved by a swift-moving river below; that the sea had already claimed hundreds of Chesapeake islands and would soon take these islands, too; that, geologically speaking, he'd shown up for his islands' last dance.[146]

It's not likely much of that figured into Hardenberg's calculus. He just liked the seclusion, the absence of urgency. He was taken by the windblown trees, the flitting birds, the shellfish at arm's reach—life's simple appearances without man's heavy hand.

Like all the bay's islands, Watts and Little Watts harbored abundant life. Shallows teemed with creatures, marshes held reeds and small mammals. Uplands—somewhat of a misnomer because they're often no more than a foot or two above sea level—furnished sufficient habitat for large and small game, trees that bear nuts and fruits, and other useful plants. Islands are integral to the unending annual rhythms of shorebirds and migratory fowl.[147]

Native Americans saw the ecological bounty in islands, including Watts Island. They didn't stay year-round, though. The biting insects were too much to bear in warmer times of year. So the islands figured into a seasonal cycle of sustenance. Tribesmen exploited island resources during cooler parts of the year but moved inland during warmer months where more bountiful harvests were to be found, giving islands an opportunity to regenerate what Indians had taken. It was a good system, one that proved reliable for countless generations. And then came the Europeans.[148]

White folks liked islands, too, although their priority on settling them seemed to be shaping these detached lands in the image of the fields they'd left behind in Europe. Islands' soil and access to the sea were attractive attributes. When Hardenberg arrived on Watts Island with the halfhearted intention of doing a little farming, he was following a long agrarian tradition that began when Europeans stepped foot on bay islands. The first permanent islanders, mostly Englishmen, let livestock loose on what were effectively fenceless pastures. They plowed tillable soil to plant tobacco and other profitable crops, following the contemporary wisdom that no good land go unplowed.[149]

In the centuries that followed, islanders willing to turn soil and tend flocks made a decent living and, in some cases, good money. By the late nineteenth century, Kent County, Maryland, alone had some three million peach trees. One of them, on Eastern Neck Island, was thought to be the largest in the United States, its trunk a robust sixty-seven inches in circumference and nearly twenty-two inches in diameter.[150]

In fact, Watts before Hardenberg held "immense flocks of sheep and cattle, with the extensive orchards of pears, figs and plums," according to a visitor there in 1884. Those were some big shoes to fill, but Hardenberg was apparently not up to the task. He brought farming equipment and a pair of horses to plow the fertile soil. The beasts should've gotten nervous, though, when Hardenberg unloaded crates of books and carried them into his new home. For his first decade of solitude, that's evidently how Hardenberg passed his days. Caring for the needy horses seemed to be the last thing on his mind. The farming hardware collected dust. The horses never had a chance; they died soon after he arrived on the island.[151]

Hardenberg's brown thumb was no life-or-death issue for him, given the bay's other opportunities for sustenance. He husbanded the already-fruited farmland around him. He was especially fond of dried figs that came from previous inhabitants' fecund fields. He put up enough of the small, brown fruit to see him through long Chesapeake winters. He'd stock up, too, on canned goods on once-yearly visits over to Onancock, Virginia, or Crisfield, Maryland, both on the Eastern Shore. Canneries were abundant on the bay's shores, a way to give bountiful harvests a long shelf life. And, of course, Hardenberg had another pantry of endless measure: a teeming estuary, right at his doorstep. And that, more than all else, is what built Hardenberg's little island community and so many others along the length of the Chesapeake Bay.[152]

The island villages born of their connection to the bay are now a dying breed. These are places where the salt tides are at the very heart of the community, where young men follow their fathers and grandfathers onto the water, where some adolescents look forward to one day captaining their own boats and others dream of escaping to the mainland. There were once scores of these communities until, one by one, people forsook them, or their isolation vanished with steel and concrete ribbons connecting them to a far shore that was once accessible only by boat. Today, Tangier Island and Smith Island are the only ones inaccessible by car that have year-round communities.

Island villages pulsed with the bay's natural cycles: the run of the shad, the shedding of crab shells, the migration of waterfowl, the influx of fresh melt water from distant peaks. Time on islands was measured not in days and weeks, but in day and night, hot and cold, tides and seasons. Living there demanded a personal connection to the bay, intimate familiarity of the nuances. Given the right tools and an opportunity to use their knowledge, islanders found they could not only survive on the bay's bounty, but profit, too. These villages flourished.

Hardenberg had no interest in making money from the waters around him, but he, too, learned to read the bay's cycles. He looked for the return of the osprey every year—a harbinger of spring's arrival, and the crabs and fish that would soon follow.

Watts, like all the Chesapeake islands, was a nursery for the life that flourished there, for the ruggedness that taming tenuous lands required, for the communities in which watches weren't necessary because life unfolded on bay time. That's what so attracted Hardenberg to his remote home, about as far from the hurried Jersey City streets as it was possible to be. Hardenberg fell in love with Watts Island, with island life. Staying ten years, as he had promised, would not be a problem.

In 1913 the government saw little reason to pay for a lighthouse keeper on Little Watts Island when Hardenberg, by then clearly a permanent resident next door on Watts, was able to do the job just as well. The lightkeeper left, and Hardenberg became the lamp's official tender. He eventually moved out of the old farmhouse on Big Watts and into the government-built home a couple hundred yards south on Little Watts. It was a big change in size, but the isolation stayed the same.[153]

Hardenberg's new place had the folksy, vernacular architecture so common to bay communities. The home was brick and two-storied, simple, tin-roofed. A front porch allowed Hardenberg the pleasure of feeling salty, summer breezes. Brick fireplaces at each end warmed long Chesapeake nights. And, of course, looming feet away was a white, brick, forty-eight-foot tower warning captains of the long shoals surrounding the islands. Little Watts was a fraction of the size of the island he'd just left—described by people who saw it as the size of a Tom Thumb golf course, a baseball infield, or a city lot, certainly no more than a couple acres. But acreage was of little concern to Hardenberg. When he needed to stretch his legs, he'd row to Big Watts. And it wasn't the land Hardenberg was concerned with, but the solitude.[154]

Hardenberg relished the solitary life. He'd wile away the hours doing this or that or nothing at all, reading, fishing, crabbing. "I liked the life from the start. It was so quiet and there was no one to bother me," he said. "My little Eden," he called it. The routines of island life sculpted Hardenberg's muscles and bronzed his complexion. He looked like a movie star, bore an uncanny resemblance to Gary Sinise.[155]

Hardenberg loved his new life so much he couldn't give it up even when he tried. In 1920, at age forty-five, Hardenberg decided to leave his island kingdom and return to city life. "I have regained my health; I have won a wage[r] that I couldn't remain away from men and women for ten years. I am going back now to my people—a new man," he announced when he left. He sold all the possessions he had brought with him and said goodbye to his hermitage. Only, he didn't. Once back on the hurried urban streets, the slow pace of the island, his home, beckoned him. He moved back to his islands once again, and this time his solitude was even more profound. He took few possessions and no books.[156]

Hardenberg's return to the islands, his retreat there in the first place, was not some paranoid break with reality. All along, he never lost his urbanity or sophistication. Mainlanders who had occasion to meet him on his rare shore calls remember him as gregarious and sharp, a cheery and good-natured fellow. Once a group of people on a large pleasure craft decided to pay Hardenberg a visit. As they rowed a dinghy toward Little Watts, Hardenberg dashed inside his house. The visitors were confused until he re-emerged as the rowboat pulled ashore, clean-shaven for their arrival.[157]

What called to Hardenberg were all the pleasures of island living, a home far removed from the cutthroat world where the ambitious trampled the meek, away from the increasing regimentation of day-to-day living. More than anything, he valued the islands' seclusion. Solitude, he once said, was the "greatest medicine a man can take."[158]

Many people had long adored islands for their distance. Pirates, Confederates, and bootleggers were among the scofflaws who valued islands' seclusion. Roger Makeele, a fearsome raider described by contemporaries as being of "evil fame" and "very bad life and conversation," used Watts Island for a time to terrorize ship captains in the mid-bay. Elsewhere, unscrupulous oyster boat captains imprisoned shanghaied immigrants in makeshift prison camps. Tippity Wichity Island in the St. Mary's River was home to Happy Land, satisfying three vices in one location as a combination brothel, casino, and saloon.[159]

Of course, not all those who enjoyed the solitude afforded by islands were on the wrong side of the law. Some just saw their isolation as a chance to try something different, to engage that entrepreneurial spirit that has driven Americans since early on. On Poplar Island one entrepreneur launched a plan to raise black cats for the undersupplied fur market in China, a scheme that failed when the bay froze and the pussies escaped—or turned cannibal and ate one another, depending on which source you believe. Another forward-thinking tycoon released a herd of Sitka deer on James Island with the intention of selling their antlers in their native Eastern Asia where they were believed to be an aphrodisiac. Like their white-tailed cousins, Sitka deer are good swimmers. Today southern Maryland has a healthy herd descended from that original group.[160]

Most island pursuits were far more mundane and had a more direct and intuitive relationship with the bay. Like Hardenberg, islanders were tied to the water; it figured into life's day-to-day exploits, sustenance, recreation, and travel, for instance. It was a way of life that appealed to people for the simple pleasures of island life—the organic smell that soft breezes sweep off marshes; the whoosh of fowls' wing beats on their descent to still water; the shades of red, pink, and purple that greet new days and nights; the silken spindrift that gives soft body to the air of seaside villages.

Even the thought of such a romantic existence was enough to have people pining for the romance of island life. In 1930, a journalist named Bert Richards paid Hardenberg a visit and that August published an article that was syndicated in papers all over the United States. The write-up painted Hardenberg as a happy-go-lucky hermit who relished in the simple pleasures of his idyllic isolation—"a life of endless solitude," Richards wrote. Hardenberg "keeps no dogs and three chickens are the only other living creatures there."

The reporter described a man whose basic needs were well-furnished. Hardenberg relied on canned goods, the article noted, but there was a more primal edge to his diet, too. "[W]hen he gets tired of canned goods," the article explained, "he catches a few fish, or takes up a few oysters from the rocks a few feet in front of his door."

The article made no attempts to conceal Hardenberg's spartan furnishings and simple lifestyle. Richards listed the house's modest inventory in its entirety: a bed and a rug, a folding card table, six folding chairs, and a rocker. Hardenberg had no books, no radio, and didn't read newspapers. His stimulation came solely from his isolation—and one game after another of solitaire. Hardenberg figured he had worn out five hundred decks of cards on the island.[161]

It would have been weeks, months, perhaps, before he heard of the Great War's armistice, of the first talkie—*The Jazz Singer*—hitting the silver screen, of the Wall Street Crash of 1929. In an era becoming increasingly accustomed to instantaneous communication Hardenberg knew he was an oddity, quirky. That living on this island, any island, meant, at least in 1930, sacrificing modern convenience as the price of isolation. Still, he wanted none of it. Which is why he must have been as surprised as anyone when, after Richards's article about him hit national papers, fan mail started pouring in.

"Charles Hardenberg, the hermit of Watts Island, was a visitor in Onancock Wednesday," reported the *Eastern Shore News* in October 1930. Hardenberg entered the office of the paper and asked for a copy of the August 15th edition—the one that had carried the local syndication of Richards's article. "You know, I got letters from all over the United States following that write-up," he told staff there. "One was from a bishop in St. Louis." Quite a few other letters were marriage proposals.[162]

The public absolutely ate him up. The question is why. What resonant chord did Hardenberg strike with a depression-plagued populace? Was it his rejection of jaded city life, of the tough bits of mainland living?

Among those who admired Hardenberg's odd lifestyle was a middle-aged divorcée named Katherine Seipel, whom he'd known growing up in New Jersey. The old friends' love blossomed through old-fashioned pen-and-paper correspondence, and in August 1931 they married. Mr. and Mrs. Hardenberg—he fifty-six years old, she forty-seven—had big plans. On the marriage registration he had listed his occupation as "writer." He planned to dictate a memoir of his life as a hermit on Watts Island to the new Mrs. Hardenberg, a former clerk and typist.

As for their island home, the newlyweds planned a major development. Mrs. Hardenberg had her eyes on the uninhabited, three-hundred-acre Watts Island next door. It had been more than two decades since anyone other than her husband had lived there. She envisioned tilled fields, livestock, and a more modern home. Together they would create their own island paradise.[163]

After all, the dry land under their feet, Little Watts Island, was becoming smaller daily. They had a couple acres at most. On Watts, they'd lay down in green pastures, reap bountiful harvests. It was an age-old dream of a prosperous future—hopeful, bright, achievable, and vulnerable to exactly the type of random bad fortune that came along in 1933.

For all the satisfaction that drew people to these islands, times were not always easy-going. Weather was a constant challenge. Sometime each autumn, the first truly cold wind blew off the Chesapeake—the one that caused recipients a momentary shudder, compelled them to gather the loose folds of their clothes around them—signaling the coming of the cold season. Hard winters, the kind that are rare anymore, created broad sheets of ice that made shellfishing, the mainstay of islands' cold-weather economy, impossible, and severed access to the rest of the world.

Hardenberg found himself in trouble this way at least twice. The first was just a few years after he moved into his first residence on Watts. He was frozen in with supplies running low. He sent out a distress signal he'd arranged with the then lighthouse keeper on Little Watts, a red blanket hoisted on a pole. The keeper was powerless to aid, but the people of Tangier Island, five miles west, responded to Hardenberg's cry for help. Long accustomed to these bitter seasons, they had plenty to spare, and hardy islanders trekked over the ice to deliver him a sledful of food and warm clothes.[164]

The folly of ill-preparation struck home, and when a deep cold spell descended on Watts a decade later, Hardenberg was prepared. Ten weeks the weather kept Hardenberg holed up. Ice carried his boat away and scuttled the possibility that some brave captain could save him. When the floes receded, boatmen went to Hardenberg's home expecting to find him dead. But this time, copious dried figs, along with a sack of flour and lard, had been his salvation. He was down to just a few spoonfuls of food when help arrived.[165]

If islanders could get through the bleak winter months, the balmy salt breezes that blew off the Chesapeake the rest of the year were one of the earthly delights that made them forget those long, hard winters. But even those were a mixed blessing. For one, they breathed life into biting flies and insects that had hibernated all winter long. At the first warm breeze those pestilential creatures shuddered to life, resuming their relentless attacks on any exposed human skin.

Those bay breezes, too, were legendary for their stormy moods, for kicking up microbursts that whipped the atmosphere into a frenzy. John Smith found this out on an exploratory voyage of the Chesapeake Bay in 1608. He and fourteen subordinates, as well as all their provisions, were crammed into a shallow-draft shallop, kind of like a barge with sails, probably thirty feet long by eight wide. Captain and crew were sailing northeastward up Virginia's Eastern Shore on a hazy and hot June afternoon. To the north, Smith saw a group of islands that included what would eventually be named Watts and Tangier and gave orders to make for them. They'd not be reaching those islands that day, though: "Ere we could not obtain them," remembered Smith, "such an extreme gust of wind, raine, thunder, and lightning that with great daunger, we escaped the unmerciful raging of that ocean-like water."

The squall forced the wet and storm-battered crew to abandon their efforts to explore the islands until the next day and camp onshore. During the Chesapeake's warmest months, such squalls are as frequent as they are unpredictable. Two days later another storm hit—this one violent enough to take off their shallop's mast and sail.[166]

But even those quick and violent thunderstorms paled in comparison to the destructive potential of the Atlantic's hurricanes. Hardenberg and his wife, even without a radio or any instantaneous contact with the world beyond Watts, would have known on the evening of August 22, 1933, that they were in for a rough go of things. Gray clouds were making wide arcs across the sky. A southeasterly breeze blew warm and steady. Mr. and Mrs. Hardenberg hunkered down. That night a driving rain began to fall.

The storm that bowled over the Chesapeake the following day—remembered as the Hurricane of 1933 since such storms were not named then—was one of the most destructive on record, the hardest to hit the Chesapeake region in all of the twentieth century. Winds were steady in the fifty-mile per hour range and gusted to eighty. The real damage came with the storm surge, though.

With the storm surge ten feet above normal low tide, it's likely that their island home was washed over. Hardenberg and his wife were forced to flee the island. Other island communities were likewise completely covered by the destructive sea. The couple moved to Harborton on Virginia's Eastern Shore to let the waters recede and the sediment settle. The landscape of Watts Island no doubt changed dramatically.[167]

But something else had changed, too: the zeal the Hardenbergs had for one another, the big dreams they had for their lonely islands. Perhaps the terror of riding out a hurricane on a deserted island was too much for Mrs. Hardenberg. Or maybe the novelty of living apart from society wore off after two years. It could be that Mr. Hardenberg realized she didn't care to share his solitude. The couple's love cooled. Soon after they took refuge on the mainland, Charles Hardenberg moved back to Little Watts Island. His wife stayed ashore. She eventually moved into the county almshouse where she lived out her days apart from her husband.[168]

Mrs. Hardenberg wasn't the only islander whose trepidation compelled her to head for the mainland. The same was the case all over the Chesapeake Bay. In fact, a general exodus had started around 1910, when many islanders realized that the thin ground beneath them was no match for climactic forces they couldn't control—an unending slate of cold snaps and stormy weather, predictable only in the sense that islanders knew in which season they might arrive. By then, too, islanders had seen the bounty of the bay, once thought limitless, crippled by unrestrained exploitation. In the 1880s, for instance, Maryland's oyster harvest reached fifteen million bushels annually. Some two decades later, despite laws that imposed license requirements, leases, and cull limits, that catch had been reduced by a third or more. For roughly a century, legal watermen from Maryland and Virginia battled, sometimes violently, against oyster pirates over oyster grounds.[169]

For Hardenberg, who had all the figs he cared to dry and money to buy canned provisions, lean years were merely an annoyance. For islanders without other means to get by, however, declining stocks left few other options. Folks floated their earthly possessions to shore, including the homes they'd known all their lives.

Despite his financial cushion, Hardenberg was powerless to stop the relentless sea. Ever since arriving on Little Watts, he'd seen the waves marching ever closer to his front door. He'd watched whole chunks of land vanish into the incessantly pounding surf. He knew it wouldn't be much longer until there was nothing left of his small island and its big brother to the north. The specks of land he'd grown to love, that were all his own, that he'd given the world for, would soon be claimed by the water.

Perhaps it was merciful that he didn't have to witness his island home's destruction firsthand. An illness forced him from his home in early 1937, and he went to his brother's place in Jersey City, where he died. Obituaries on the Eastern Shore lamented the void Hardenberg's passing left, that residents would no longer see his smiling face on his rare visits to the mainland.

For Little Watts Island, Hardenberg's home for the last twenty-nine years of his life, the end came in 1944, seven years after he died. A storm that autumn undercut the bank supporting the lighthouse. The following year, it toppled into the waves. The bricks are now incorporated into a home in Onancock.[170]

Little Watts Island is one of some five hundred documented Chesapeake Bay Islands that have been lost to the sea. Scientists estimate that all the bay's islands that now exist will suffer the same fate by the year 2100.[171]

On a balmy fall morning, I went looking for some scant trace of Charles Hardenberg. I hitched a boat ride to Watts Island with a Virginia Department of Wildlife Resources biologist named Jeremy Tarwater. There's no trace of Little Watts—it's completely washed away—but I nevertheless held out hope that Hardenberg left some footprint on Big Watts.

The skiff bounced along the bayside creek as dawn broke. To our sides, watermen pulled crab pots, working the last few weeks of a decent yield before cold water came. Tarwater rounded a marshy finger that reached westward into the bay from the Eastern Shore's mainland and Watts Island came into view, bathed in pink morning light.

Tarwater moderated the throttle—even the eight or ten mile per hour headwind threw the waves into a bit of a choppy tantrum, so he laid off it some to save our legs and bottoms from the repetitive slapping of hull on water. Still, we were going pretty fast—probably ten knots or so—and it took us about fifteen minutes to make it out to Watts.

The boat motored into Watts's lee, Tarwater eyeing suitable spots to anchor. He circled the island once for good measure, but that brief tour of the island's western edge confirmed what he already suspected: even that ten-mile-an-hour breeze kicked up waves far too rough to anchor on the windward side. What struck me most was that the day was actually pleasant. I shuddered at the thought of the lashing the bay gave Watts during an angry mood.

Biologists like Tarwater are among the few individuals who are permitted to walk about on Watts. After the island was willed out of Hardenberg family hands, it had a succession of absentee landowners until the United States government acquired Watts and folded it into Glenn Martin National Wildlife Refuge. State and federal biologists occasionally do bird counts on Watts. Law enforcement patrols from time-to-time. Laws prohibit trespassing, but locals have been known to stretch their sea legs on Watts when government employees aren't watching.

Tarwater and I hopped out of the boat. Telltale signs of the people who had once lived here were everywhere and nowhere at the same time. Large swaths of the interior are vast carpets of English ivy. People brought this fast-growing plant to Watts long ago. When man surrendered his dominion here, the opportunistic vine took off. Ivy shrouds 150-year-old trees and reaches in many spots to the water's edge. If there is a human footprint someplace underneath, it is buried by the ivy they brought here. Other than the vines, there is no sign of the generations people spent here.

Where ivy hasn't claimed ground, wild grapes grow. Underneath old trees' canopies, the grape vines are spindly, the fruit and leaves spare, enough for the birds who now call Watts home, but a far cry from the conical clumps that dangle prettily from tenderly tended stock at vineyards.

The most striking feature of Watts today is the active erosion occurring there. The mild northeast wind—quite modest in terms of bay breezes—whipped the waves into enough of a frenzy that they crashed into Watts's western shore with sufficient force to send sizable spray into the air with each wave. Whole clods of the island's sandy earth sloughed into the bay. Full-sized trees lay toppled, or nearly so, at the interface of the shore and Watts's upland. The shoreline is retreating so quickly some of the toppled trees still have green leaves.

Sandy shoals appear at mid-tide at Watts's north and south points, stretching a couple hundred yards into the bay. They disappear at high tide. They used to be firm ground, undoubtedly ground Charles Hardenberg once walked without a care in the world. On one of these flooded hummocks is a sign that warns people to stay off the island. Soon there'll be no need for those signs and the insatiable bay will turn its attention to larger islands and the communities there, and those islanders' footsteps, too, will one day soon be buried at sea.

Chapter 8

Anthracite Coal Towns: Communities Consumed by Undying Fire

Late one Saturday evening in 1915, coal miners underneath the western slope of Wilkes-Barre Mountain in Pennsylvania were ready to call it a day. They looked forward to a Sunday off, an opportunity to recharge their overworked bodies. But their respite wouldn't arrive without a final hiccup. A mine car had toppled over, a problem they needed to correct before heading out. A crewman hung his carbide lamp from one of the timbers that were framed at regular intervals to keep the roof from collapsing. By the dim glow of golden light, the team righted the unwieldy beast, their week's labor finally complete. The men left the Red Ash coal mine. The lamp stayed behind.

More than a century later, the ground is still on fire.[172]

In what was once Laurel Run, Pennsylvania, scrubby hillsides vent gases made hundreds of feet below the surface. There, deep in the bowels of the Earth, smoldering seams of coal still burn. Through fissures in rocks on the surface, steady cushions of steam roll into open air. Several old vent pipes, like rusting candy canes buried nearly to the crook, pour heat that wrinkles the view behind them.

Those pipes are one of the few manmade signs that people have been here, taken stock of what resides far below, considered their options, and decided to let the inferno burn. They're also a symbol of man's feebleness against the forces of nature. The fire below draws humans to scale, paints us as a reckless and impulsive lot. An anomaly along Earth's long timeline.

Our enduring love affair with coal has had unintended consequences, among them climate change and landscapes permanently altered to mine the rock beneath. Another effect that rarely garners notice beyond coal country are the numerous fires that smolder in the mines we abandoned. They will be burning long after our dependency on coal has come and gone.

Northeastern Pennsylvania is a couple hours' drive from both Philadelphia and New York City but a world away. The terrain ripples in long, sharp ridges that cast deep shadows over narrow valleys. This landscape moved a lot over the past few hundred million years, tilting and squeezing the few long beds of coal that underlay these valleys. All that pressure compacted the rock, making it the super-shiny, tough-as-nails, ultra-carbon-rich coal called anthracite. It takes a lot to ignite this dense coal, but once it gets going, the anthracite burns hot and long.[173]

Wend your way over this region's snaky roads and you'll eventually see firsthand just how reliably anthracite can hold a flame. The borough of Centralia is a grid of empty and overgrown streets that would resemble some post-apocalyptic town were it not for the notable absence of all but a few structures. But the ghost town is not so much the attraction here as the wasted hillside overlooking the empty borough. A few hundred feet from the impeccably maintained St. Ignatius Cemetery is a charred slope of baked rock. Standing sentry are the skeletons of trees killed by the noxious fumes venting from holes that have opened in the ground. The buried fire creeps west at a glacial pace.

People who have heard of long-burning coal mine fires at all have likely heard of Centralia, where a 1962 fire in a landfill, which was an old strip mine on the edge of town, ignited seams of underlying anthracite. The coal has been burning underground ever since.[174]

State officials tried to extinguish the burning seam at once. They flushed the landfill and adjacent coal. They tried to create a barrier of non-combustible material. They tried to dig an enormous trench to contain the fire. Nothing worked, and the smoldering seam continued to burn, inching its way outward beneath the surface.

The fire under Centralia grabbed residents by the lapels in 1981 when a hole opened in a resident's yard and swallowed a boy. On Valentine's Day that year, twelve-year-old Todd Domboski noticed wisps of gas puffing from the base of an ash tree and moved closer to investigate. The earth opened and took him in whole. Domboski's salvation was the quick sense to grab onto a root exposed by the sinkhole. A cousin leaned into the steamy abyss all the way to his waist to grab hold of Domboski's wrists.[175]

The saga of the mine fire pitted neighbors against one another, split between those who wanted the government to bail out residents that had seen their property values vaporize and others who thought the fire posed no threat to their lifelong homes and preferred to stay put. Centralia made international headlines. Eight months after the earth swallowed Domboski, Centralia residents appeared on *Nightline* with Ted Koppel. Media came to town from around the world to investigate so peculiar a phenomenon as an inextinguishable underground fire. Centralia residents understandably became media shy.[176]

But all that exposure paid off. Federal authorities relented, and Congress authorized $42 million in funds to buy the property of all of Centralia's eleven hundred residents and resettle them elsewhere. There were some who wouldn't be moved at any price. Well into the twenty-first century, there are holdouts who refuse to leave, fire or no. Many insisted that the buyouts were little more than a ruse, an effort by the government and coal companies to get at all the unmined, unburned anthracite underneath the town.[177]

A few houses still stand, and they're occupied by those hangers-on. The government refused to strong-arm those who wouldn't leave. Now they're lone sentinels in a vanished borough. All around them are the skeletons of the borough's past life: an ornamental bush, a line of hedges, a depression that was once a driveway. But the houses are mostly gone.

This was once a blue-collar hamlet, a proud borough that was that quintessentially American, a mix of hardscrabble immigrants and their descendants, Irish Catholics and Eastern Europeans, who had found decent work and decent lives among these fields of anthracite. Humble beginnings prepared them for the challenges of eking out a living in the coalfields, but nothing could have prepared them for a fire that swallowed people whole.[178]

Today, curiosity draws to Centralia people who want to see the spectacle of an underground fire that's been burning for more than sixty years, a span of time that's both long and trivial. The same year this fire started, Chubby Checker's "The Twist" hit the top of the Billboard charts, the Cuban Missile Crisis came to a head, and the Limbo was all the rage. People have to stretch their memory to summon that time if they're able to stretch their memory that far at all. Still, geologically speaking, sixty years is nothing. It's an instant compared to the time it took to make the coal fueling that fire.

Seams of coal have been burning since humans first stumbled into civilization millennia ago, and likely long before that. Scientists estimate that Australia's Burning Mountain has been on fire since 4000 BC. Germany has its own burning mountain, or Brennender Berg, that's been ablaze since 1688. Even in the frigid reaches of Canada's Northwest Territories, the seaside Smoking Hills contain coal seams that have been smoldering for centuries. Seams that outcropped needed only a lightning strike or a wildfire. Sometimes the mixture of fuel and air provided the right conditions for spontaneous combustion.[179]

Unmined seams of coal readily burned inward if the face caught fire. They still do. The solid rock ignites and turns to ash, creating a retreating face that offers the fire a steady, unbroken source of fuel along which it slowly burns. But it was the introduction of organized and substantial coal mining that offered the perfect recipe for coal fires to take off.

West of Richmond, Virginia, is a diamond-shaped basin of coal that French Huguenot settlers discovered in 1699. By 1819, when *American Journal of Science* correspondent John Grammer visited Richmond's coal "pits," as they were known, there were at least twenty-five shafts that descended as far as 350 feet below the surface (a depth that would more than double in years to come). Far below ground, laborers, mostly enslaved people, worked the damp and gloomy subterranean tunnels with little more than pickaxes, lit only by the dim glow of candlelight.

At the Black Heath mines, Grammer wrote that "part of the coal was on fire: I could not ascertain when this fact was first observed to exist; and it is not impossible that the coal may have been burning a century, or more." The smoldering blaze vented on the side of a hill. "Attempts were formerly made to extinguish the fire, by turning water into this hole," wrote Grammer, "and, after every attempt, there was a temporary disappearance of the smoke for several weeks; but never longer than three months."

Richmond's coal pits illustrate the reason human intervention made coal seams rife for fire. Open flames provided illumination in coal mines, and volatile gases built up underground, resulting in blasts that killed people and lit the workspace ablaze. And mined seams—by their very nature—leave behind a network of tunnels that feed a steady stream of oxygen to the voracious blaze. Flushing often didn't work because natural drainage patterns, complicated by the network of tunnels, meant the water followed the path of least resistance. It moved in the direction of gravity, not people's wishes.[180]

The story was the same across the country, with abandoned mines burning almost every place people tunneled into coal. In the 1930s, young men enlisted in the Civilian Conservation Corps logged some 1.6 million hours just fighting coal fires. CCC Camp 886, based outside Gillette, Wyoming, was tasked exclusively with extinguishing the coal fires there.[181]

So the mine fire that ignited under Centralia three decades later wasn't an anomaly. It wasn't even unique for Pennsylvania. There are currently more than a hundred documented underground coal mine fires in the United States and perhaps thousands worldwide.[182]

What was special about Centralia's fire was where it burned: smack dab under city streets. Most coal mining, and thus most mine fires, occurred away from populated areas, and because there weren't people packed in tightly, most mine fires were simply ignored. Centralia's fire, however, crept underneath homes and businesses. Dangerous levels of carbon monoxide and other lethal gases slithered into peoples' homes, sickening them and making them lose consciousness. This was part of the reason the federal government eventually coughed up funds to buy Centralians out.

But even in its claim to fame—a ghost town made by a mine fire—Centralia was not alone. By the time residents began leaving Centralia for good, a couple places had already long since been evacuated because fire singed their roots. Carbondale, Pennsylvania, was the site of the first deep anthracite mine in the Northern Anthracite Coal Field. Carbondale, it turns out, provided a blueprint for Centralia twenty years later. The strip-mine-turned-landfill in the gritty town's West Side neighborhood caught on fire in the 1940s. Officials dropped the ball. They tried to douse the fire. They tried introducing fire resistant material and excavated a trench. Nothing worked, and sadly, two elderly residents of the neighborhood over the fire died of asphyxiation. In 1960, the government bought out and relocated a thousand residents.

The mine fire is still likely smoldering, though it no longer threatens people and their homes, and state officials believe they have contained it. And while this history is an indelible part of the city's history—Carbondale Area High School Chargers play ball where coal seams once burned—even Carbondale was a late comer to the mine fire scene.[183]

Joe Gregory and I walked into the wooded slope at the base of Wilkes-Barre Mountain, unsure if what we were looking for would even be there. After all, it had been fifty years. "The only way you can tell where people's homes existed is by looking for the oddball trees they had in their yard," Gregory said. He moved with his family to Laurel Run as a five-year-old in 1940 and lived here until he left for college.

Gregory, who died in 2022, was trim and spry. He didn't take himself too seriously and was self-deprecating at every opportunity. He paused occasionally to look around in this early-spring forest and get his bearings. There were glints of recognition, despite fifty years of growth, and the familiar landmarks urged him onward. We were on South Dickerson Street, where Gregory grew up, but there were few obvious landmarks to speak of, other than the oddball trees he still recognizes. Only in thin irregular patches did the leaf litter betray a glimpse of the street's cracked, thin asphalt.

But Gregory urged me to look a little closer, to look beneath all the undergrowth, and set Laurel Run's skeleton free, if only for a brief moment. Property lines jumped out of the forest, showing boundaries that separated one lot from the next. Walls stacked of flat slate tell of residents who long ago buffeted the terrain against erosion down this slope's natural contours. The erstwhile borough's detritus appeared at first to be forest litter, when truly, under the veneer of moss and lichen, laid a vehicle's rotor, or the stained porcelain of a toilet or a post still holding fast to its concrete anchor. And there from the mottled brown forest floor bloomed parallel lines of daffodils, planted with an eye for design decades ago.

Gregory still saw old Laurel Run. He gestured up a hill, and I followed his direction along what was South Dickerson Street, now just a sloping hallway through the forest, covered by a vaulted canopy of branches. "My house was just up there," he said. "My wife, future wife then, lived just across the street."

But even shooting for an approximation of the layout was all but impossible. Gregory's childhood home was long gone. His wife's is too. So are the other 160-odd structures—houses, a school, a church—that government officials razed in the 1960s. Unlike in Centralia, there were few holdouts. And even those who did muster the courage to stand and fight didn't stay too long. When other measures failed, all the buildings in Laurel Run were bulldozed into a pit and torched. But the borough lives on in many ways, including in Gregory's memoir, *Home Town Gone.*[184]

When the Red Ash coal mine underneath Laurel Run caught fire in 1915, the company that owned the mine tried to put out the blaze by inundating it. At first, it seemed to have worked, but six years later, the smoldering seam flared up once more. For decades, miners worked around the fire, sealing off passages known to be ablaze, mining coal in adjacent seams.[185]

All the while, the gases from the fire vented through Laurel Run, and Gregory said that the mine fire was just a fact of life. "It smelled like rotten eggs, but it was something we were used to, it was just there," he said. "In March we would go fly kites on the side of Wilkes-Barre Mountain, and we would stand beside the vents to stay warm."

It was a simpler time, a more innocent time, Gregory remembered. "There was very little crime. We had one policeman. His pay was fifty dollars a year and bullets." Indeed, more than twenty years before Gregory's family even showed up, Laurel Run sold the prison cell hardware it kept in the town hall because there was no need for it, so peaceful was the community.

Laurel Run was a collection of homes both humble and proud, narrow clapboard houses and cinderblock garages. On the main street, mom-and-pop shops sold staples and simple pleasures. Like much of the rest of the anthracite coal fields, the sixty-five or so acres of Laurel Run were a tight grid of narrow streets, rimmed by imposing mountains. "I'd go up the hill to pick huckleberries to sell, which usually didn't work because I'd eat them on the way down," Gregory said. "There was one of everything in town, so whatever it was, it had a simple name: the creek, the school, the borough."

Laurel Run was "a God-fearing community of believers," said Patricia Hester, who grew up in Laurel Run but now lives in Washington state. "The higher streets were mainly Protestant, and those nearer the railroad tracks were mostly Roman Catholic."

Hester's upbringing in Laurel Run was so potent, that she, like Gregory, felt compelled to write a memoir. But she found her remembrances infused with so much dramatic ebb and flow, what began as a memoir became the novel *Whispers from the Ashes*, which chronicles the day-to-day struggles of the Branigan family as the town vanishes around them.

"The men were mainly blue-collar workers in heavy manufacturing jobs. The women were wives and mothers. Few worked outside the home except in the typical female jobs—nurses or teachers. Because the roots were deep and few secrets were kept, there was also a lot of gossip over back fences," Hester said.[186]

One reason that petty squabbles resembled family bickering, Gregory said, is that many neighbors were related. Gregory kept three-inch binders full of photographs and other mementos he collected from his hometown over the years. He pulled an old bulletin dated 1922 from the only Protestant church in town, Laurel Run Primitive Methodist Church. He thumbed through the faded pages listing the church officials and participants in this week's service. "He was my cousin," Gregory said. "Oh, and she was too." In that single bulletin, he identified at least ten people he was related to by blood or by marriage.

Mining underneath Laurel Run stopped in 1957, along with Red Ash Coal Company's efforts to contain the fire. The residents of Laurel Run had known all along, of course, that a mine fire burned under their borough, but other than unpleasant odors, the direct effects had largely stayed out of town. Within several years of the coal company's departure, however, noxious gases seeped into people's homes and forced them out. Snow melted on the ground in many spots above the mine fire. Residents' porches separated from their homes, which often made an eerie creaking sound as wood settled into new positions. People started to get sick. Plants started to die.[187]

Three levels of government got involved and came up with a plan for putting out the fire and moving residents out of harm's way. By 1965, the Luzerne County Redevelopment Authority had taken over the task of relocating Laurel Run's 850 residents. Gregory said that some wanted to stay. A few had been born in their homes and wanted to die there. But this was an era before late-night TV came to town, an era before flashy lawyers used their media presence to threaten their will into happening. "People just accepted the fact that they had to leave, whether they liked it or not," he said.[188]

Hester remembered that Laurel Run's fire "was just as acrimonious as the Centralia fire, but censure and good manners meant the fight stayed within the community." There was little publicity. One contingent hired a lawyer to fight with what little money they had, but not much came of it. By the early 1970s, Laurel Run's residents were all gone, their homes, businesses, and municipal buildings razed.

Mining engineers had done what they could to extinguish the underground fire, boring holes to determine exactly where it had spread, digging a trench, and inundating the old mine. Like previous attempts to put out the fires, those efforts didn't work. Even today, there's no end in sight. Estimating how long a mine fire will burn is incredibly tricky because there are so many factors to consider—the rate of burn, or the location of groundwater, for instance. Experts surmise there may be enough coal for Centralia's fire to burn for 250 years. It's not inconceivable that the old Red Ash coal mine could smolder that long, too.[189]

It's easier today to find the mine fire than it is to find the physical traces of Laurel Run. Gregory said that the razed homes were pushed into a big hole and burned, a poetically tragic fate for structures made obsolete by a fire that never actually touched them.

Though fire indirectly took all the traces of places like Centralia and Laurel Run, it wasn't able to sever the ties people had to their homes. It's in memory and connections that people keep these towns alive. When the borough of Centralia opened a time capsule in 2014, many former residents showed up to pay their respects. Laurel Run's residents have likewise shown their affection for home through a play and a novel. They share memories on a Facebook page. Their affection for the place is genuine and enduring. For all the strife and struggle of living in a vanishing community, nothing can break the bonds to home.

"Some places have monuments to all the notable citizens they reared or are known for famous things," Gregory said. "We had a fire."

Chapter 9

The Abandoned Pennsylvania Turnpike: Apocalypse as an Attraction

"This all started because William Vanderbilt was pissed off," said Murray Schrotenboer, my guide for a bike trip on a glorious autumn morning in Pennsylvania's Southern Alleghenies. It was an odd thought. William H. Vanderbilt, son of legendary captain of industry Cornelius Vanderbilt, was a robber baron and philanthropist in his own right, sporting titanic mutton chop sideburns, and remembered, above all, for grandeur: railroads and shipping lines, mansions, libraries, even a university, all decked out in Gilded Age splendor. Try as I might, I found it hard to summon the industrialist on this stretch of forsaken highway.[190]

The road is hardly an example of obscene wealth or conspicuous consumption in its present condition. In fact, it screamed quite the opposite. Trees were growing where pavement should have been. The asphalt was cracked and settled in many places, leaving gaping potholes. Leaf litter in some spots had accumulated so thick it resembled a forest floor. The claim of Vanderbilt's excess, bad mood or not, hardly bridged the gap between the Gilded Age and what was before us.

But Schrotenboer was onto something. As the owner of Grouseland Tours, a family-run mountain bike guide service in south-central Pennsylvania, he's been pedaling this path for years and knows its history, how this morphed from a robber baron's vendetta to a wasteland. It's the Abandoned Pennsylvania Turnpike, a thirteen-mile stretch of highway that's been closed to commuter traffic since 1968. Despite this road's age and apparent neglect, though, it's a gem among abandoned American infrastructure, because all this crumbling asphalt is a special and accessible peek into another world through a cracked looking glass. As we started our journey on the eight and a half miles that are open to cyclists and pedestrians, the bright autumn sun warmed our backs. Schrotenboer, along with a cast of users ranging from day trippers to film producers, see beauty in the neglect, promise in the decay. And that optimism might be a good plan for reuse of this and many other abandoned places.[191]

The sun doesn't shine on all of the Abandoned Pennsylvania Turnpike. Parts of it are in tunnels. The builders of this path had to move mountains to achieve what they wanted. At the time, the shafts they bored through solid rock were an accomplishment worthy of admiration. But those tunnels later proved to be this beleaguered stretch's undoing. The fact that they are shielded from the sun that nourishes overgrowth on the rest of the road may ultimately, and somewhat impossibly, be their savior.

I met Schrotenboer at the southern terminus of the Abandoned Pennsylvania Turnpike in Breezewood, Pennsylvania, which, in a sense, is an iconic American town, a slice of apple pie in the Alleghenies. This isn't by virtue of being some Mayberry-like, sleepy hamlet tucked among the patchwork of Dutch-settled farms, though Breezewood was once that. No, Breezewood happens to lie at the junction of Interstate 70 and the Pennsylvania Turnpike, so it is stuffed to the gills with gas, restaurant, and lodging chains. It's the United States' love affair with automobiles and fast food, wrapped in a tidy package. It's this kind of unbridled capitalism, that good old entrepreneurial spirit, that goaded Vanderbilt into the pissing contest that would eventually result in the Abandoned Pennsylvania Turnpike.

The story begins in the nineteenth century, when officials from the Pennsylvania Railroad had the audacity to offer competition to Vanderbilt's New York Central Railroad with a competing set of tracks in the Empire State. Vanderbilt, usually known for his level-headed business decisions, uncharacteristically lost his cool and wanted revenge in western Pennsylvania, planning new tracks through the Alleghenies to bite into his competitor's monopoly there.[192]

Vanderbilt spared no expense, enlisting titans of business and industry, such as Andrew Carnegie, to help finance his plan. Southern Pennsylvania's rugged, mountainous terrain was no barrier. His men surveyed a winding route, forcing a locomotive-friendly grade into the tricky terrain. Where mountains stood in the way, he punctured them, boring nine tunnels. As many as 6,500 laborers, mostly immigrants, blasted and graded. Dozens lost their lives. Stonemasons built bridge piers across the Susquehanna River and laid culverts over every gurgling stream that crossed the proposed path. Some of that masonry still sits in Pennsylvania's rural game lands, sturdy as ever, peeking through a delicate blanket of moss and fallen leaves, silent testament to Vanderbilt's plans.[193]

Eventually cool heads prevailed, no doubt because money flowed through this project like a sieve. Vanderbilt had burned through $5.7 million of his backers' money (certainly a nine-figure sum in modern dollars) when the project was about two-thirds complete. That changed Vanderbilt's mind. He pulled the plug on the South Pennsylvania Railroad, and it became "Vanderbilt's Folly." Left behind was a right-of-way through the Southern Alleghenies, long stretches of railroad-friendly grades and six tunnels in various stages of completion.[194]

Schrotenboer filled me in on the life and death of this ill-fated project as we set out on the first leg of the Abandoned Pennsylvania Turnpike. While it was hard to make the leap from all the Gilded Age shenanigans to the present, it was possible to appreciate the grade Vanderbilt's locomotives required to pass through the Alleghenies. In a vehicle, a steep hill means merely inching the pedal closer to metal. On a bicycle, though, the same incline demands an effort that's likely to leave riders breathless, their thighs begging for mercy. But on this first stretch of the abandoned road, there was none of it. The old turnpike is pancake flat.

Blindfolded, you'd be hard-pressed to guess you were in the Allegheny Mountains. While the grade is barely noticeable, if at all, the road follows the contours of the adjacent mountain, changing direction a couple times. But even these curves require effort to notice. They're long and gently arcing, the kind of change that one hardly notices today as the world whips by the window at seventy miles per hour.

I didn't even notice them on a bicycle. Instead, what caught my attention were the stunning views of the valley below that appeared when the surrounding forest opened up. In fact, I only became aware of the curves when Schrotenboer pointed them out. "It's these features we take for granted on modern roadways," he said, rousing me from my comfortable wonder. "These low grades and gentle curves."

These features were exactly what visionaries in the golden age of the automobile had in mind when they set out to build one of the nation's first modern superhighways. The long spine of the Appalachian Mountains, extending from Maine to Georgia, had long vexed east to west travelers. Even when automobiles entered the scene, good roads across the mountains were scarce, and the few that existed were tangled ribbons of pavement that often led to rollovers, skidding, and crashes.[195]

In 1935, Pennsylvania lawmakers created the Pennsylvania Turnpike Commission and charged the body with creating a superhighway that overcame the challenges of dangerous roadways. They wanted to do away with hairpin turns and brutal slopes, some of which exceeded nine percent grade. Fortunately for the commissioners, there happened to be just such a route that had been collecting dust for more than four decades. That's why this road was so revolutionary; it was a broad, flat tarmac at a time when most roads more resembled tangled shoestrings.[196]

It's the reason, too, that Schrotenboer and I were able to glide along almost effortlessly. The turnpike had been constructed in the late 1930s with all the gusto of a New Deal project. Some seventy million dollars of federal money poured in, and so did fifteen thousand men eager for the work. The 160-mile highway was ready in two years, astonishing by any standards, but missing an important deadline by just a couple months.[197]

"The turnpike wasn't on time," Schrotenboer said. "It was supposed to open on July Fourth with reporters, bands, and ribbons. Wasn't ready. They pushed it back to Labor Day with bands, reporters, and ribbons. Wasn't ready. So they decided to have a quiet opening because there were no other holidays. It's not like they were going to do it on Halloween. They decided for October one. People lined up at the toll gate so that they could be the first ones to go on this new superhighway. The first car was let on and it went twenty feet before reporters stopped it to ask what it was like to ride on the first superhighway. Everyone else behind him had to wait."

Schrotenboer and I stopped for a breather, not because we had to, but because he wanted to show me something. He scrambled uphill, up the side of the road and, impossibly, found a flat patch on an otherwise sloping mountainside. "This is it," he said. "This is the reason for the whole thing—the railroad grade."

It was hard to make out after a hundred and thirty-odd years, but sure enough, there was a wide, flat grade, broad enough for a railroad track or two, slowly surrendering to the forest. The turnpike follows the general path of the old railroad—or what would have been the old railroad. At some points, the original grade was simply widened to accommodate four paved lanes. In other spots, that grade was visible parallel to the roadway, as Schrotenboer showed me. And elsewhere, the railbed was off in the forest and couldn't be seen without a considerable and dangerous trek in the woods.

But there are a couple points along the Abandoned Pennsylvania Turnpike where the railbed and the roadbed are one and the same. After hopping back on the bikes and gliding once more along the turnpike's kind grades, it turns out there was one of these overlaps just around the gentle curve. And unlike the easy trek up to that point, it was scary as hell.

Had we been standing at the mouth of Rays Hill Tunnel seventy years before, there would have at least been some illumination. Schrotenboer tried to calm my apparent trepidation by offering the tidbit that the lighting would have been puny by today's standards. "They had mercury vapor lights every fifty feet, which didn't offer much illumination," he said. "There were postcards showing these tunnels brightly lit when in reality there wasn't enough to see."[198]

That's small consolation given the total darkness that was before us. On my tiptoes, I could see a minuscule speck that was the other entrance, but there was a three-quarter-mile tube of darkness to get to the light at the end of the tunnel. Even the light from lamps Schrotenboer had affixed to the handlebars of the bikes were swallowed by the darkness. Schrotenboer had a well-practiced routine for getting through the tunnel. "The best thing to do is stay in single file and look straight ahead. Keep the light twenty to thirty feet off and just look straight ahead," he said.

The tunnel was chilly, musty, and wet—exactly what you would expect inside a mountain. What was a gentle breeze outside became concentrated and gained leverage inside this tube, offering some resistance for people trying to pedal through it. "Once I was guiding a group through here and the wind was kicking so hard that a lady couldn't move against it. It was like the blades of a copter: whump, whump, whump."

Or maybe like the engine of a locomotive, as the case may be. This was one of six tunnels left over from the South Pennsylvania Railroad that turnpike planners opted to keep. As these tunnels were among the project's more difficult aspects, the builders of the Pennsylvania Turnpike put them to use, more or less as-is, with one lane of traffic in each direction and no median separating them—a design that would turn out to be a fatal flaw.

I was relieved after a short ride, the far entrance growing and casting ever brighter light. I was even more relieved to feel the combined weight of my flabby body and steel bike frame fly from my pedals. Though the slope was almost indiscernible with a casual glance, what was before us was unmistakable. We were coasting downhill, picking up steam with no effort at all, letting gravity take over.

The ride thus far had not been too grueling; it was flat virtually the entire way, but I was grateful for the break, not only because it offered respite to legs that had known too much driving and not enough biking, but also because it offered a few moments of reflection, a context that may not have arrived had I been focused on my underworked thighs.

As we coasted downhill, gravity worked in our favor and our bodies split the air like jelly. The whoosh made conversations near impossible as the roadside foliage whipped by in a blur. I realized this must have been the same sort of exhilaration sensed by passengers in some 1940s-era jalopy, windows down, tasting the sweet mountain air.

How fast they must have thought they were going. How free they must have felt from the constraints of the lumbering, laborious world. It was a wartime era of confidence and expectation, when major achievements and victories made it seem like virtually anything was possible. Planners thought that motorists would be able to take the curves on the Pennsylvania Turnpike going seventy miles per hour. Initially there was no speed limit, and drivers routinely pushed the speedometer to ninety.[199]

And while those rosy predictions were a bit optimistic, their dreams marked the thinking of a new era, the automobile age, the infancy of America's love affair with cars, a dalliance that would prove soon enough to be a lifelong, complicated relationship.

Ahead we slowed to wait once again at the entrance to a tunnel before proceeding into the dark abyss. This one, the Sideling Hill Tunnel, was longer—one mile. So long, in fact, that I couldn't see the other side. It's not that the tunnel curves; the Sideling Hill Tunnel is ramrod straight. There's a slight arch in the floor that peaks midway through, and with the tunnel's length, that slight rise is enough to conceal the distant entrance. Instead of that opening being a far speck in the distance, it cast a faint glow on the tunnel's ceiling like a ghost, stuck there in the mountain for all time.

Today, making the harrowing journey through the Sideling Hill Tunnel, or any part of the Abandoned Pennsylvania Turnpike for that matter, costs little more than the sweat of your brow and the courage to descend into a spooky abyss. Long ago, however, motorists traversing this road paid money—a penny a mile. Organizers weren't sure if people were going to pay such an exorbitant sum. There were, after all, alternative routes. Rough and winding, true, but without tolls. Yet people proved they were willing to pay in a big way. The road reached capacity well ahead of projections.[200]

It was a novelty in those days, a modern highway as we know it. It was faster and safer. No more hairpin turns or steep grades. Motorists got across a dangerous landscape, all while going through as many as seven mountains. And there was a convenient, added benefit of taking this route: fast food.

Schrotenboer and I coasted our bikes to a stop at an open expanse the size of a city block that sat atop the Abandoned Pennsylvania Turnpike's westbound lanes. The blacktop had been bleached white from seventy years of sunbathing. Scraggly growth rimmed the rectangular expanse. A dense copse of trees and growth grew in the middle like some bedraggled and forgotten cemetery. And in a sense, it was. This was the Howard Johnson's that once occupied center stage of this travel plaza.

By the time the turnpike opened in 1940, HoJo, with its signature orange roof, had more than a hundred restaurants. This commanding presence, along with its acclaim for fast, consistent food, helped the chain secure a contract to serve all of the Pennsylvania Turnpike's travel plazas.[201]

Travelers could get HoJo's Ipswich Clam Plate with Tartar Sauce for fifty cents and a hot fudge sundae with nuts for a quarter. Salads, cold cuts, steaks, and chops were all on the menu, and travel-weary diners could fill themselves up and be on their way.[202]

That copse of trees is no longer recognizable as a HoJo except for the incongruous tiles that still cover the middle of the travel plaza. We had reached our midpoint, our stopping place, where we turned around and headed the other way, and there was no place more appropriate than this, a pitstop where countless drivers once pulled in to take a load off, recharge, take a momentary break from all those kids nagging, "Are we there yet?"

We headed back toward the Sideling Hill Tunnel, and Schrotenboer pointed out a fact that might be lost on those not looking for it, the whole reason that planners surrendered this stretch of road. At each of the tunnels, the Abandoned Pennsylvania Turnpike goes from four lanes down to two. They're bottlenecks.[203]

"It doesn't take a genius to figure out that going from four lanes down to two would cause problems," Schrotenboer said. "The backups were as much as five miles long. I was leading a tour group and one of the men on the group remembers being in a backup for an accident in the tunnel and it took five hours to clear it. Something had to be done."

The turnpike commission doubled four of the seven tunnels to make two more travel lanes and avoid the possibility of head-on collisions. But in the case of three others, the only option was a bypass. Thirteen miles of the Pennsylvania Turnpike were abandoned when that bypass opened in 1968. Two of the tunnels are open to the public. One is off limits and used for high-speed aerodynamic testing by an automobile racing organization.[204]

What happened after that was Mother Nature doing her thing, tentatively at first, with more vigor once she established a foothold. An endless freeze-thaw cycle has cracked the pavement. The fringes of the roadway today are lined with the successors to the emerging vegetation, in many cases fifty-year-old trees that happened to sprout as saplings when traffic was diverted from this stretch. Ailanthus, or tree of heaven, has taken hold in many spots, as it has on many American roadways. An apple tree still produces pretty fruit near the remnants of a rotten and leaning Civilian Conservation Corps building. They're both from a time when people had a very different relationship to this road.[205]

Though the Abandoned Pennsylvania Turnpike is a relic, it's not frozen in time. The road is beholden to the sun and the seasons, ever changing, decaying, returning to a wild state of nature. But not all of the turnpike is like this. At one end of the Sideling Hill Tunnel, Schrotenboer told me we were stopping for a spell. The flat portals were wedged into the surrounding faces of the steep slopes like a dam. These facades were very dated, and not just because they've encountered neither wrench nor paintbrush in forty years. There was something about their styling, their feel, that conjured the past, like a living room set from *The Brady Bunch.*

Schrotenboer pulled out a few granola bars, ostensibly the reason for our sojourn, but as it turns out, we were also pausing to let a large family move on. He didn't want them following what we were about to do. One of the young men in the party moseyed up to a door at the side of the tunnel's entrance. There, a freshly painted gray metal door, bearing no doorknob but deadbolt evidently secured, blocked his path. He tried vainly to squeeze a couple fingers between the jamb and the door. No luck. "Aww, man," he complained. "You can't go in there anymore."

"No matter how hard he tries, he's not getting in that door," Schrotenboer mumbled. Which turned out to be right, because as soon as the family went on their merry way, he pulled a key from his pocket, turned the deadbolt, and heaved open the door.

These were the Sideling Hill's control rooms where the nuts-and-bolts of keeping the tunnel operational occurred. High up above were glassless windows that let in the muted light of the forested mountain. They also allowed precipitation to enter, covering the floor in a permanent layer of water, rusting every metal surface in the dank, enclosed space, including a staircase that Schrotenboer ascended cautiously. We passed a boiler room, coal cascading out of a storage chute, frozen in that moment for forty years.

We stood beside a massive industrial fan that once circulated fresh air through the tunnel. Bits and pieces of the control room made their way off over the years, Schrotenboer said, either by wear and tear or by sticky fingers. The tunnels used to have signs that proclaimed their names, for instance. But the fan was so big, its components so cumbersome, that it stayed put.

Schrotenboer slinked through a doorway and down a few stairs, beyond the flimsy light of the broken windows, and into the darkness beyond. By the light of our detachable bike lamps, I could see that we had entered the sliver between the tunnel's ceiling and the top of the arch. The slabs we were walking on were the tunnel's roof. Holes here and there were once used for lighting and ventilation. We paused to take it in. The silence was total. We saw a lone bat, content in the dark and quiet. Schrotenboer said that more than a dozen species of bats use these tunnels. When the weather flips and the air outside the tunnel becomes colder than the air inside, the bats show up in droves.[206]

Water seeped through the round walls of the arch in places, but there was little decay. With no sunlight here and a consistent temperature, the natural forces turning the turnpike outside to dust have found no purchase here. Hidden from the world, the tunnels may be the longest-lasting piece of the Abandoned Pennsylvania Turnpike. That's the beauty of these tubes. They'll be here long after the humans who made them are gone, shielded as they are.

The same, unfortunately, can't be said for the portion of the Abandoned Pennsylvania Turnpike that is exposed to the world. But not if Schrotenboer can help it. He and several acquaintances were leading an effort to make the Abandoned Pennsylvania Turnpike a regional attraction by making it more bike and pedestrian friendly. To this day, it's a use-at-your-own-risk trail locally known as the Pike 2 Bike.

For a long time, no one was quite sure what to do with the Abandoned Pennsylvania Turnpike. While it was derelict and decaying property of the Pennsylvania Turnpike Commission, it became a hotspot for partying teens. Remaining graffiti and beer cans offer testament to these uses.

The government used it for military training exercises and as a proving ground for all those features of roads we take for granted. Traffic engineers tested road reflectors here and tried out five different designs for rumble strips, the milled depressions that make a jarring buzz when a vehicle is leaving a roadway. Safety engineers tested reflective paint, bringing in old folks to test it, and asking them which ones they could see and which ones they couldn't. [207]

The Abandoned Pennsylvania Turnpike has even been used a couple times for the silver screen, for a scene in the end-of-the-world independent film *The Road* as well as a B-grade zombie movie.[208]

But the most organic, the most public use, according to Schrotenboer, is precisely the way we saw it, with the sun on our backs, the wind coursing through our hair, the dank tunnel air chilling some sense into us. When that happens, you feel free, like you're coasting through time, through the mountains that human ingenuity has leveled, or at least overcome.

"Some of the people have said 'Well when we clear some of the trees away from here and plant flowers in the median . . .' and I'm thinking, they just don't get it," Schrotenboer said. "This is a singular spot, there is no other place like this. This is post-apocalyptic America."

Chapter 10

The New River Gorge: When Nature Returns, Aliens Do, Too

One after another, they jumped into the void. Occasionally a momentary pause interrupted the steady stream, but there never was any hesitation. They bounded willingly, many gleefully, over the edge and into thin air. Nearly nine hundred feet below, they landed in water and on dry land, even occasionally getting tangled in a tree. Thousands of onlookers stood by and watched, peering over the side, observing each jumper's fate.

Framing this spectacle was a backdrop of stunning beauty. The New River Gorge is a distinct "V," a canyon that cuts hard through the Appalachian Plateau, forming a natural funnel that descends to a thin ribbon of rushing water. It's like the gorge calls to you with open arms, beckoning you in. And you can indulge its plea—with enough training.

Every year authorities in Fayetteville, West Virginia, close the New River Gorge Bridge—the only high-speed span over the canyon—so that BASE jumpers (that's building, antenna, span, and earth) from around the world can legally practice their daredevilry on the third-highest bridge in the United States. Visitors flock to Bridge Day every October to witness this Mountain State festival.[209]

The bridge's vital statistics are impressive. It's the longest steel arch bridge in the United States, coming in at 3,030 feet, six inches, and weighing more than forty-four thousand tons. But it's what the bridge traverses that's even more remarkable. The New River Gorge is sometimes called the Grand Canyon of the East. Under the right conditions, Bridge Day syncs up with peak fall foliage. Forget New England; leaf peepers come from all over to appreciate the autumn scenery, and local businesses are all too happy to accommodate them.

During the best weekends, passenger trains snake through the gorge for the sole purpose of admiring the fireworks of fall.[210]

Yet the visible splendor of the New River Gorge is only veneer; underneath the canopy lay human footprints of a century exploitation, dozens of ghost towns built for the purpose of taking the gorge's usable resources. Crumbling stone walls, rusted metal skeletons, and fallen headstones remain as mute testament to a century-long endeavor that fueled the nation's growth.

If those inorganic footprints were all that people left behind, the gorge would have had little problem folding them back into its embrace. But along with all those manmade artifacts are relics that once grew among gorge residents—living, reproducing organisms that didn't yield as easily as the structures people left behind.

Non-native plants found firm footing among the gorge's abandoned towns, and so, oddly enough, the return to nature wasn't exactly a return to a *natural* state. What the New River Gorge has become is an illusion of sorts, not the pristine, natural wilderness one might assume from a cursory glance. Woven into the white oaks and rhododendrons is a compromised landscape, one in which invasive species vie with natural vegetation for a foothold in the reclaimed landscape. The gorge is an ongoing lesson in how—or how not—to return a place to nature.

After learning of the New River Gorge's storied history and the ghosts that still reside there, I decided to encounter the remains firsthand. Today the New River Gorge National Park and Preserve offers a network of trails that affords adventurous sorts the opportunity to get up close and personal with this rich landscape.

On paper, the Kaymoor Miners Trail seemed suitable. It begins at the rim of the gorge and, after a handful of switchbacks and stairs, ends a mile later at river level. All along the way, there are traces of the past. From the turn of the twentieth century until 1962, miners extracted nearly seventeen million tons of coal at the mine called Kay Moor Coal Mine No. 1, and the community of Kaymoor thrived around this bountiful production. When the coal seams were exhausted, so went the town, and for five decades, nature has been growing over the community that was left behind. The Miners Trail snakes through the deep time that created the gorge, and the relative instant that people lived there to exploit it.[211]

Early on I took notice of warnings that the Miners Trail was strenuous and shouldn't be tackled without due diligence. But I shrugged off this admonition. After all, I'm a seasoned hiker, fit enough, and I reasoned that my ambition for getting this rare peek into the past would trump any vertical obstacles. That was my first mistake. My second? Bringing along a hiking "partner." But hey, my son has been on a lot of hikes with me, and he was a real go-getter of a five-year-old.

I brimmed with warmth and optimism as my son Shane and I held hands on a crisp October day at the trailhead, looking down to the rushing current nearly one thousand feet below. The hike, I was sure, would illuminate hidden ghosts of the past, not to mention that it would be a father-son bonding moment long remembered and cherished.

We stood there on a slab of concrete, peering down into the chasm we were about to enter. That platform, it turns out, is part of what's left of Kaymoor's haulage. Kaymoor, like several other gorge towns, existed in parts at different elevations. At Kaymoor bottom, along the train tracks and river, sat residents' homes along with the community buildings and all the infrastructure necessary to process and export coal. About midway up, on a flat level called Sewell's Bench, were the mine portals. And at the rim was Kaymoor Top, a small cluster of homes and businesses with roads leading to points elsewhere.[212]

The haulage was a means of moving people between these locations. It was a two-car affair, each the other's counterweight. When one went up, the other down. The haulage moved on tracks and was anchored by the stout concrete platform on which my son and I now stood, a platform that should have served as an omen. Even gorge residents, seasoned mountaineers well-acquainted with hoofing it up and down hills, knew that tackling the gorge's steep slopes was not for the faint of heart.[213]

The reality check to come was not yet apparent, and for the moment, we stood there. I was blissful in our ignorance, watching the water below, considering how long it would take us to get there and back, and musing on what minuscule fraction that would be compared to the amount of time it took the New River to get where it is today.

You'd never guess by name alone that the New River is ancient—at least three million years old and possibly a hundred times that, the modern version of an old river system called the Teays. One theory suggests that the river got its incongruous name from a cartographer who had never recorded it before and so called it the New River.

The New cuts across the Appalachian Plateau rather than following natural contours of ridges and valleys—one clue to its advanced age—as it meanders nearly 320 miles from its sources in the highlands of northwestern North Carolina and through Virginia, all the way until it merges with the Gauley River to become the Kanawha River in central West Virginia.[214]

Over those millions of years of coursing along, the New cut through strata of rock, gouging a gorge that reaches a maximum depth of sixteen hundred feet. In a sense, Shane and I were following the river's vertical path as we descended into the gorge. The autumn air took on a decided nip as we left the sunlight and walked into the cover of the forest canopy. A foot-wide stream of water cascaded over an outcrop, wishing us luck as we went on our way.[215]

From the middle of the New River Gorge Bridge, the gorge looks like a broad "V." Put your boots on the ground, though, and things don't seem nearly so gentle. As a matter of necessity, the Miners Trail begins with seemingly interminable switchbacks that zigzag downhill so that the slope is manageable. What is a hundred vertical feet becomes ten times that when you must move your body that distance. The grumbling from my fair-weather outdoor buddy began in between the first zig and zag.

The geological processes that made this canyon are still hard at work. The New River carved this gorge through several types of sedimentary rocks such as shale and sandstone. Although vegetation, leaf litter and a thin layer of soil blanket much of the gorge, rock shows its face in many places. Rainwater that swells the fervent river drips over these cliffs nonstop, weakening rock a little at a time. Part of the face periodically falls away, crashing its way downhill until encountering something big enough to stop it.[216]

The trail in many spots is littered with these jagged castaways, making firm footing hard to find. I tightened my grip on my boy's hand, as much to keep him steady as to prevent him from stepping off-trail and rolling downhill.

On a golden-retriever-sized hunk of shale that had recently come to rest in what would have been the trail's straight path sat a fit couple who could've stepped straight from an outdoor clothing catalog. They were on their way up. "Hello!" I boomed, still eager for the challenge that lay ahead. The man, head down, elbows resting on his knees, offered a single raised finger in reply. The woman looked our way and forced a smile. She did a doubletake at the sight of Shane. Without a word she looked back at me, searching for an explanation. Wondering. Accusing.

Her wordless admonition steeled my resolve, and Shane and I soldiered on. From below on the next switchback I heard her mutter a feeble warning: "There are a lot of stairs down there."

By the time I knew this was a stupid idea to try with a five-year-old, there was no turning back. My ego wouldn't permit it. But Shane's would, and just like that, not yet halfway into the downhill portion of the hike, he announced he'd walk no farther. He would play along on this foolhardy venture, sure, but only on my shoulders. I effectively became an ass.

Needless to say, our arrival at Sewell Bench was a welcome respite, as much to take a load off as to explore the interface where hundreds of miners left the known world for the bowels of the Earth each day. There, halfway down the slope, is another layer of sedimentary rock: coal, the compressed remnants of organic matter that lived and died in a boggy quagmire lacking the oxygen needed to completely decompose. And it was that coal, thin as those strata were, that would abruptly and radically change this gorge.

Though coal has increasingly been the subject of scrutiny and scorn, we are nonetheless addicted. Roughly twenty percent of the electricity generated in the United States comes from burning coal, and that proportion used to be far higher. As of 2020, the United States consumed nearly 477 million tons annually. That's more than eight pounds per person, per day. This love affair is nothing new. American coal mines produced the potent fuel source by the eighteenth century, but much of the coal was dangerous and difficult to get at. Americans knew of the vast reserves of Appalachian coal. "In the western country coal is known to be in so many places, as to have induced an opinion, that the whole tract between the Laurel mountain, Missisipi [*sic*], and Ohio, yields coal," wrote Thomas Jefferson in *Notes on the State of Virginia*, published in 1781.[217]

Producers were licking their chops to get at the coal seams beside the New River. Unlike the underground mines to the east, these seams outcropped on the gorge. Mining that coal was, in many cases, a matter of cutting a portal straight into the canyon walls. But without a means of transporting New River coal in any measure, those seams were all but worthless other than to keep mountain pioneers' home fires burning.[218]

Chesapeake & Ohio completed a main line astride the New River in 1873, and the gorge changed overnight. Businessmen and land speculators bought up tracts that had once been worthless. Miners cut portals wherever seams would allow. Towns sprang up overnight to house and feed the hordes of men and their families that came to the gorge to work in the mines.[219]

They were little towns with funny names like Echo, Alaska, Prince, and, yes, Kaymoor, often sandwiched on the thin sliver of land between sheer cliff and river. Train tracks always ran through these towns—their way in and out, their lifeblood. [220]

The owners' or foremen's homes, as well as the company store, were often stout structures made of cut stone. Ramshackle clapboard homes covered the buildable parcels not reserved for those buildings necessary for the mines to function—the powerhouse and tipple, for instance. Often a long stretch of real estate near the tracks was reserved for coke ovens that belched sulfurous smoke twenty-four hours a day, blanketing the town with a perpetual haze of gloom.[221]

Often, seams of coal that were minable—anything at least twenty-four inches thick was worth a go—were located up along the gorge wall, halfway or so, where there wasn't much flat earth for living space. There'd be a few support buildings but not much else at the portals where miners descended into the earth. Coal that spilled from the mouth tumbled on a tipple downhill to awaiting rail cars and shipment to distant furnaces.[222]

And while coal barons were at it, many took the virgin timber that covered the gorge walls. That, too, was in constant demand, not only in their own gorge towns, but also nationwide. Soon enough, the gorge was as far from a virgin landscape as it was possible to be. Over the course of twenty years, two firms, Sewell Lumber Company and Babcock Coal & Coke, harvested all available timber on some forty thousand acres adjoining the New River Gorge.[223]

In the New River Gorge, everyday dramas played out, most of them mundane, the travails of humans trying to eke out a living in a harsh world. But there were remarkable moments, too, that interrupted the humdrum of life in the gorge. Major disasters occurred with unsettling regularity: forty-six miners died in an explosion at Red Ash; 114 perished in a blast at the Layland mine. And that's to say nothing of the roof falls and accidents that killed and mangled miners one or two at a time.[224]

For all those incidents that still cause heartache, there were moments of levity, too. One mine owner named Paddy Rend consolidated several mines only to turn around and sell his holdings for $1.2 million, a sum beyond wildest imaginings back then. Upon receiving his check, he walked over to the nearest bar, bought the house a round of drinks, then boarded a train, never to return to the New River Gorge. And that bar where Rend shared some of his earnings, at the Dunglen Hotel, was reportedly the site of the longest continuous game of poker, a fourteen-year match that was brought to a halt only by West Virginia's prohibition on alcohol.[225]

Especially remarkable is the larger picture, what that coal did for the nation at large. From the time in 1873 when coal began spewing from portals by the ton, the United States' industrialization was on a tear. New River coal burned in the boilers of locomotives that moved across thousands of miles of new track. That coal fed naval assemblages, as with Teddy Roosevelt's Great White Fleet, which spread American power and influence around the world. That coal was responsible for the steel mills that girded bridges and skyscrapers, iconic structures such as the Empire State Building and the George Washington Bridge in New York City. New River coal was in some way part of every American victory and failure. New River coal fed the United States' coming of age.[226]

And all of that, every single bit of it, sprang from these tunnels that were cut into the side of the earth. Making that clear, preserving and interpreting those world-changing realities, is a worthy goal. It's nevertheless hard to muster that deep perspective, much less any perspective, standing at Kaymoor's bench level. There are evocative ruins there: an intact powerhouse, the cut stone shell of a mining office. And, of course, there are side-by-side portals, low-slung arches almost any adult would have to crouch to fit inside. Standing at the edge of the portals, fitted with iron grates that allow bats to come and go while keeping unwanted critters (including *Homo sapiens*) out, the dank air is cool and musty. Weeds grow over a vehicle that carted coal from this very hole many decades ago. The whole affair would normally inspire reflection, but it was a hard time coming as I stood in that spot.

For one, I had on hand a five-year-old who seemed attracted to the site's dangerous features, among them steep drop-offs and sharp, rusty metal. But I realized on second thought that he did offer some perspective. Toting thirty-five pounds of dead weight made me cognizant of the burden of physical work, even though it was nothing compared to what miners endured inside those tunnels, blasting and shoveling tons of coal, day after day, by the dim light of a feeble lamp.

Still, I felt like there should have been some sort of in-the-moment, transcendent connection to the past here, but it just wasn't there. What's more, I noticed something a little off, out of place, a real problem taking over the ruins I was hoping would transport us back in time: tree of heaven.

Ailanthus altissima, despite its common name, is anything but heavenly. The tree first arrived in Philadelphia as a transplant in 1784 from its native China. The tree appears pleasant enough; the gray bark is smooth and thin, the feather-shaped, alternate leaves resembling fat versions of palms. In its native range, tree of heaven can grow to heights of seventy feet. The tree has long been used in traditional Chinese medicine.[227]

As recently as the twentieth century, folks gushed over the tree's tendency for fast growth and hardiness. It was especially prized as a city tree since it was capable of eking out a living in bleak ground. The tree's tenacity was a central metaphor for poverty-stricken city dwellers in the 1943 classic novel *A Tree Grows in Brooklyn*. Even *The New York Times* heaped praise in May 1950: "Here is a tree as citified as a subway and, surely, it is nearly as rugged. It thrives on the lack of nourishment in the city's parched paved area. It breathes in smoke and industrial gases and automobile exhaust in quantities that would kill its country cousins." Tree of heaven, claimed the newspaper, provides "pleasure for those who welcome its shade and special beauty."[228]

Beneath tree of heaven's charming doggedness, though, lies an invasive species that's a real son of a bitch. For one, it's fast-growing. Seedlings can shoot up six feet or more in their first year, a rate of growth that is in many cases three times faster than native species such as oak or maple. The tree sends out long lateral roots that snake through soil and work into the crevices of masonry, bulging and cracking surrounding material as it grows. An individual tree can produce upward of three hundred thousand seeds. And if tree of heaven's lush foliage, rapid growth and fertility wasn't enough to shade out competitors, there's a kicker, too. Tree of heaven makes a toxin that poisons other plants—a wolf in sheep's clothing.[229]

Tree of heaven cannot tolerate a lot of shade and so is often found in a part of the ecosystem that many different creatures rely on for sustenance: edge habitat. That's why, in the thirty states where tree of heaven is known to exist, there are long stretches of highways that are lined by the species. Normally that interface between woods and open space, especially in a maturing forest, is a fortified pantry, offering ample cover and food for many different species. But when tree of heaven, which has little value for North American wildlife, comes to dominate a space like that, a normally rich part of the ecosystem loses many of its assets, and organisms are forced to look elsewhere for provisions.

There's little use trying to kill tree of heaven with any means short of poison. Take a chainsaw to the base of the trunk and you merely piss it off. Multiple shoots will emerge from those long roots and a new trunk will start growing from the side of the old one. Eliminating tree of heaven once it's established requires loads of time, effort, and money.[230]

And that's what felt a little off about Kaymoor's bench level—that there was an interloper there, that it wasn't entirely *real* wilderness coming back to reclaim what men left behind in the gorge, that this was somehow compromised. If I needed motivation to finish the hike, the tree of heaven at Kaymoor's bench level furnished it. The palmy leaves, brilliant red in their fall dress, spread their crowns and drank in as much sunlight as they could on the rim of the clearing. Trunks shot up from the craggy masonry, branches overhung the ruins of the old coal car repair shop. I resolved to descend to Kaymoor proper far below and wander a landscape more along the lines of the evocative reclaimed ruins I had come there to find.

Fresh motivation notwithstanding, I still had to contend with a grouchy five-year-old, not to mention the fact that I'd also have to climb back up each of the 821 stairs I was about to descend. The National Park Service installed the wooden staircase years ago to traverse the unwalkable slope. Still, the staircase didn't render the descent effortless. And I wasn't sure that I'd tackled 1,642 stairs my entire life. But I was hell-bent. Through a steel frame from Kaymoor's operational era reading "Your Family Wants You To Work Safely," I took the first step of the formidable descent.

At about stair six or seven, we were back to the Dad's-the-jackass routine. Shane insisted he was going on my shoulders or not at all. My bribes promising goodies back at the car fell on deaf ears. Probably a third of the way down I began to notice the tremble. I set Shane down on one of the flat landings that allow stair climbers to take a breather. My legs quivered at the unfamiliar workout of taking so many stairs at once. But still I pressed on, the occasional old relics—a forlorn brick shack, a rusted water tank—goading me onward. And just when I thought my legs could take no more, the rusted skeleton of a coal conveyor emerged at last, leveling out in a long arc. The end of the staircase peeked from the void. Kaymoor. Our Point B. We sat and devoured our lunch.

Kaymoor (or Kaymoor Bottom as it's more accurately known) is much as you'd expect an abandoned mining town to be. The sturdy structures that were the town's bread-and-butter are shells of themselves, but shells nonetheless: an expansive powerhouse, a tipple, all manner of metal structures, once functional, now defunct. In one part of the noble old town, five train tracks lay on the forest floor, native trees growing between ties completely blanketed by detritus. The homes where families once lived have long since disappeared, their siding and frames carted off bit-by-bit for other projects, their feeble foundations folded into the growing forest. Though Kaymoor died when the coal seams pinched out, there remain echoes from the past. Trains hauling coal from mines a couple counties over still rumble by on the tracks that front this forlorn town. And just beyond, the ancient, timeless New River casts an everlasting current of white noise across these old bones.[231]

Before commencing the long march uphill, I wanted to see one more part of Kaymoor. The coke ovens there are still, for the most part, intact. The coke ovens of the New River Gorge are, in many cases, impeccable works of craftsmanship by Italian masons whose skill remains admirable today.[232]

Finding them wasn't difficult; they were always near the tracks where the carbon rich coke could be loaded onto trains bound for northeastern steel mills. After navigating some of the same boulders strewn about that Kaymoor's workmen would have known all too well, the coke ovens lay silently just where they were supposed to be. They were impressive works of art that aged with grace because they had been so well constructed. It's almost as if you could faintly see laborers standing there, shoveling in coal to have the impurities smoldered out. But even that was a little tough; standing in those laborers' place atop the coke ovens was a long line of trees of heaven.

Shane and I took our time going uphill. He didn't even pretend to try to walk himself upstairs. He rode on my shoulders the whole way. My weary thighs burned with each step. I drew heavy, unfulfilling breaths. We stopped often. And somewhere along the way he transformed into my coach, signaling his eagerness to be done with it: "You don't have to stop for breaks," he told me.

The upshot of our (my) uphill climb was that it afforded ample time for reflection. Although I had come to see, in essence, nature's resilience, I realized what I had found was something different: a landscape that will never return to what it was before humans took root. Leaves and dirt will soon enough cover the tracks people left behind in these gorge towns, but it will forever be altered nature.

I realized that my slow slog uphill with thirty-five extra pounds of burden was a metaphor for what the National Park Service contends with in the New River Gorge. Preserving and interpreting so spectacular a national treasure that's been so deeply compromised will always be an uphill climb. But as Shane and I emerged at the trailhead at Kaymoor Top, completely spent but no more uphill climbing ahead of us, I had no doubt in my mind that it had all been worth it. We were that much richer to have had that experience together. We walked toward the car, hand in hand, passing by a gaggle of hikers just going in, buoyant, giggly, full of expectation, probably not knowing they'd be traversing a landscape that had been changed forever, an appearance that's as much a product of history as the ruins of the coal town below.

Chapter 11

Kiptopeke's Concrete Ships: A Second Life for Unlikely Vessels

The concrete ship *SS Willis A. Slater* must have been quite a spectacle steaming in reverse across the open ocean, a barn-door-sized hole yawning in its bow. In fact, the whole misadventure was such a fool's errand, the captain reckoned, that when the fickle Atlantic eventually cast the *Slater* to Bermuda instead of the American mainland as he had hoped, the broken ship just stayed there for repairs.[233]

That strange episode has been all but erased from memory. Mariners still sidle up to the immobile *Slater*, but few have any notion of some long-ago collision. Most think little of its wartime service or ponder how concrete floats or wonder why the ship ended up half-sunken with eight other identical vessels to begin with. The sailors at the *Slater* now are nearly all recreational fishermen who bob on the surface of the Chesapeake Bay, reaching out to push against the aged hull, keeping their watercraft from scraping against the rough concrete.

Few people are sure what to make of the concrete ships at Virginia's Kiptopeke State Park. The old vessels are just part of the landscape, derelict phantoms a few hundred yards offshore in two arcing rows, aligned north to south. They have been there as long as anyone can remember. Ask around and explanations run the gamut. Some folks think they were fake boats once used for bombing practice. Others have some vague recollection of their being surplus merchant ships.

The Chesapeake is both a curse and a blessing for the concrete ships. The elements are cruel and unrelenting and work with the all the persistence of a schoolyard bully to reduce the vessels to ruin. Despite their decay, however, the ships' time at Kiptopeke, more than seven decades now, has been a long bonus round after brief wartime service, a postwar gig they lucked into while so many other ships of the same era found themselves sunk, scrapped, or left for dead. By all appearances, the ships at Kiptopeke are not too far behind them.

I knew that somewhere behind those breached hulls, crumbling facades, bird droppings, and barnacles, stories lurked, waiting to be told. Coaxing those tales out of the depths proved harder than I anticipated, but once they emerged, they told of unexpected detours half the world over, of ingenuity and reuse, of a private playground for bored locals—longer, more colorful journeys than their decrepit condition now lets on.

I had paddled around these concrete ships in a kayak many times before, always with the aim of bringing home some of the Chesapeake Bay's prized delicacies: speckled trout, flounder, and especially, striped bass. At the right time of year, stripers in the Chesapeake can exceed forty inches, which is a lot of meat on the table, not to mention a photograph destined to remain a Facebook profile picture for years. My attention during loops around the concrete ships was thus tightly focused on the gentle tug that indicates a fish had finally swallowed one of the slithering eels on the end of the line. Still, in the shadow of these behemoths, I always kept one eye on the end of the reel and another on the hulls that towered above me. I'd get around to the ships' history one day, before I realized I lack one crucial element for being an outdoor writer—the skill to catch fish.

That day came one October when I showed up at Kiptopeke, sans fishing gear, to meet Ted Boelt, then the park's unofficial keeper of the concrete ships. After a long career in the Big Apple, Boelt retired to the Eastern Shore where he had family roots. When I met him, he spent his days manning the cozy store at the head of the park's bustling boat ramp. Outside of selling fishing tackle, ice, and other nautical necessities, Boelt fielded a lot of questions about the old boats just offshore, and it's easy to see why. There are nine of them, each more than 350 feet long and 54 feet wide. Much of their thirty-five-foot depth sits above the water. You can't miss them.

"The most frequent question I get is 'What are those things?'"

Boelt told me as we sat on a bayside bench with a front row view of the ships. "A lot of people think they're Liberty Ships, which they're not, but the concrete ships were just as important."

Boelt explained that the concrete ships were, like Liberty Ships, a World War II initiative and that, despite original intentions to have them haul dry cargo between North American and Caribbean ports, the fortunes of war generated new orders that saw some of them sent to the South Pacific—a theater aflame with combat. Their wartime service was just the beginning of their long careers and, sadly, their long decline. Boelt authored a pamphlet about the ships that he handed out to visitors who show more than a passing curiosity about them.

While Boelt and I talked, staccato gusts blew fine, salty mist over our conversation. Several times I swept my vision nearly 180 degrees to take in all nine ships. "They're in a sad state now," said Boelt, "but they've done a lot of good over their lives, in war and in peace. We can't get too caught up in what they once were. We have what we have. There's not really any effort to preserve them because that would take a lot of money. I think the best we can do is just to remember them. To tell their stories. That's how they'll live on. But even that is hard because so much has been lost. We don't even know their names."

"Really?" I wondered, incredulous. I thought for sure that, with the hundreds of sailors who served onboard these ships and the thousands of fishermen who have since wet a line beside them, someone at some point would've written down their names. But that didn't happen, at least not in a readily accessible place.

"We know the names of the ships that came here, but not where each one was positioned. So we have nine of them out there but can only say with certainty that the second ship is the *Thacher*."

I raised my eyebrows.

"Some time back, a gentleman came by who was part of the crew that towed the *Thacher* here. He said they almost didn't make it. There was some sort of crack in the hull near the engine room. Somewhere around Cape Hatteras—a patch of ocean called the Graveyard of the Atlantic—storms and rough seas almost forced the crew to cut the towline and let the *Thacher* go to avoid having both ships wrecked. They thought for sure the *Thacher* would sink. But it didn't. That near-disaster was more memorable for him than where they placed the *Thacher*, but he was fairly sure it was the second in line."

I was hooked by the story, not to mention the nautical nostalgia that wells up in a wannabe mariner who has never actually had to ride out a storm on the high seas. What's more, I had a challenge, a mission. I could make some discovery that someone other than me might actually care about. I told Boelt that I wanted to get up close and personal with the ships, to observe the features so often left unobserved. I offered him my spare kayak, which he politely declined. He was nevertheless excited that I'd be paying special attention to the old ships.

"Look for a name, any name, if you get a chance," he said. "It will usually be up at the bow or, more often, at the center of the stern. Unfortunately, I think all of them have faded or fallen into the water. Best anyone can tell, we've lost their names."

The sea breeze was blustery coming off the wide water, and a robust gust interrupted our parting. He turned his body away from the blow. "And be careful out there," he chided.

I promised to do my best to find any remaining identifiers and report my results. I appreciated his cautionary send-off, though offered a "what-can-you-do?" shrug in response. I was an experienced kayaker, after all, and had been in water at least this rough. I retrieved a kayak, paddle, and life jacket from my truck and took them to water's edge. I shoved off into the choppy Chesapeake.

Paddling into a headwind is like walking on a treadmill set on the steepest incline—on your hands. With each rest you give your aching biceps, the breeze erases two-thirds of the progress you made since the last break. I would have given up right away were it not for the sense of purpose that kept me soldiering though. I couldn't let Boelt down, let these old ships down, and if an hour or two of exhausting paddling was the price I'd pay, so be it.

Approaching the ships with a fresh lens for the history they represented, rather than the undersea creatures I might tease from them, I noticed at once how they betrayed their seventy years of age, how the concrete crumbled into the bay. What were once painted hulls were now dull, sandy surfaces streaked by rust that bleeds from exposed rebar. Their forms remained, but here and there, chunks of concrete the size of a book, or a sidewalk tile, or a parking space, had long since forsaken the hull and fallen into the water below.

I examined a few sterns, looking for any faint trace of a name. Nada. Zilch. Nary a letter. I decided that the windward side, then receiving the full rays of the falling sun, might better illuminate any blanched markings. I knew that leaving the broad lee of the ships would make paddling a bit more challenging; I wasn't prepared for the can of whoop-ass nature opened once I rounded the stern of the northernmost vessel.

What had been relatively healthy gusts to the east of the ships was a steady gale west. Waves that were gentle and bobbing became punchy and dangerous on the bay side. I nearly capsized twice, and made the command decision, in an effort to avoid becoming fish food, to restrict my research to the ships' leeward stretches. I aimed the kayak for a narrow gap between one ship's bow and another's stern. The incoming tide was racing through the narrow gap like a sluice and seemed eager to slam my kayak against the hull. I prepared to use my paddle to shove off the concrete, sized up the narrow breach to assess my grim chances, looked down then up. And there it was.

A number.

Right beside a hawsehole on of the bows. A short number, with an "H" at the front. H14, to be precise. Definitely not a name, but something to work with. Buoyed by this discovery, I trolled the leeward flank of the two lines of ships and found a couple more, committing their location to memory. Alas, the numbers on the sheltered side of the hulls were not all there, meaning I'd have to brave the melee I'd just left to find any other usable clues or return to fight another day. I chose the latter.

Those numbers I saw on the bows, it turns out, were so-called yard numbers given to each vessel while they were being constructed at McCloskey and Company in Tampa, Florida. And the record of the yard number belonging to each ship is widely available.

I shared the news with Boelt, and we were both excited at the prospect of learning which ship was which. We conceded that we might be among the few people to appreciate those identities, but that restoring their names nonetheless bestowed some measure of dignity to these fading pillars.

A few weeks later I convinced my wife to join me in finding the yard numbers I had missed on that first voyage. I was glad to have a buddy along, so that in the event I went into the drink, there would be someone to tell the Coast Guard where to look for me.

On shore, the day seemed almost windless. Even so, the exposed western side of the ships was once again energetic and unpredictable. A whitecap washed over my lap every now and then. Currents raced fast through the slot between ships. Certainly not a venue for the tepid kayaker. My wife Adah's admonishments evolved from gentle questions ("Have what you need now?") to firm declarations ("Let's wrap this up.") to the silent stare of death reserved for those occasions on which I have acted especially buffoonish. She claims to have nearly been attacked by a pod of dolphins. As much as I would have liked to stay and explore those under-appreciated relics, Mama had spoken. It was time to head in.

I had all the yard numbers but one, and that meant I had the vessels' names. And with those names, I had identities, and with identities, stories—of the long journeys these ships took to this singular spot in the Chesapeake Bay.

The rhetoric that led to the creation of the concrete ships sparkled with the same optimism that preceded World War I's wooden emergency fleet. Concrete vessels, claimed a correspondent in a July 1944 issue of *The Washington Post*, "have shown they can take the beatings of rough weather and still ferry the supplies to the global war fronts." They'd counter swarms of U-boats prowling the seas, offer a workaround to the wartime shortage of plate steel, help keep up a steady supply of all the fuel and foodstuffs needed to support the greater war effort. The praise for concrete ships was gushing, starstruck, as if they were the Clark Gables of the war effort.[234]

Only this was a different war, a different era, and Americans weren't going to fall for any old shipbuilding program, despite the popular president's affinity for sleek wooden yachts. World War I's wooden emergency fleet had been too disastrous. The nation was willing once again to consider an unconventional building material to help crank out ships, but this time they'd go with one that hadn't gotten the bad press that the Great War's wooden steamers had. This time, the boats would be made of concrete.[235]

Concrete merchant ships had a vocal booster club during World War I. "A Possible Solution of the Shipping Problem," the Portland Cement Association called them in a promotional pamphlet. "A Field for Pioneers," the journal *International Marine Engineering* said of reinforced concrete shipping in 1917. One wartime bureaucrat offered the rosy prediction that concrete ships would soon be "filling the ocean." Another backer even made the audacious claim that a concrete vessel hit by a torpedo wouldn't sink. Despite all the buzz, though, an experimental concrete shipbuilding program in World War I produced a fleet of only twelve vessels, all of which were completed *after* the armistice.[236]

The most illustrious of World War I's concrete vessels, *SS Atlantus*, is now a wreck, slowly disintegrating 150 feet off Sunset Beach in Cape May, New Jersey. *Atlantus* ferried troops and hauled freight after the war and would have lived on as a ferry dock had it not snapped free during a tow and run aground. So heavy and ungainly was the concrete ship that efforts to dislodge it proved futile.

There had been major improvements in concrete ships by the time World War II rolled around—namely that their hulls were stronger—and producing one was still cheaper and required less metal than a steel ship, so government officials facing shortages at every turn were willing to give concrete another look. The government's efforts first centered on concrete barges, but in 1942, Uncle Sam awarded McCloskey and Company, a Philadelphia shipbuilding firm, contracts to build twenty-four concrete steamships at a yard in sunny Tampa, where they could crank out ships year-round. The endless warm weather that would one day beckon legions of retirees to the Sunshine State meant that the concrete could cure as easily in January as in any other time of the year.[237]

McCloskey and Co. launched the ships with as much fanfare as they could muster during a war effort that, by late 1943, had lost its novelty. They brought in notables, such as the Catholic Archbishop of Philadelphia, to offer blessings and goodwill. The ships were mostly named, naturally, after men who had made significant contributions to the science and industry of concrete—like Dr. Arthur Newell Talbot, professor emeritus of municipal and sanitary engineering at the University of Illinois. Among Dr. Talbot's many accomplishments was a significant study of reinforced concrete. He did not live to see his life's work given a maritime commemoration; the *SS Arthur Newell Talbot* was christened two years after his death.[238]

While the cutting-edge research by Dr. Talbot and his colleagues produced marked improvements, it was clear that concrete retained a few vexing shortcomings. Weight was one issue. The same math that worked for steel did not for concrete. In what goes down as perhaps one of the most spectacular, if forgotten, "oops" moments in American history, the first three ships McCloskey produced suffered long cracks in their hulls at the very moment they were launched because of an error distributing ballast. The concrete ships were slow, too, and never did deliver on the architects' promised speed of ten knots. Their clunky design made for an unflattering nickname, "squatters," since the stern, where the heavy engine sat inside the hull, rode noticeably lower in the water.[239]

Concrete ships were civilian vessels designed to carry commodities like sugar from Cuba, one of countless run-of-the-mill tasks necessary to keep soldiers and society at large plugging away and, thus, supporting the war effort. And at that—hauling dry, bulk commodities—the ships were fantastic, since their holds didn't sweat inside like steel-hulled vessels, a shortcoming that ruined some of the cargo they contained. Those thick walls, however, proved a double edge sword, as they made the crewmen's quarters unbearably steamy—in some cases as hot as 120 degrees—and with a crew of two dozen sweating men, no doubt an olfactory nightmare.[240]

Decision makers faced somewhat of a dilemma with ships that, in some ways, exceeded their expectations and in others fell short, so they changed course mid-stream and reassigned the concrete fleet to duties that better suited the boats they turned out to be. The *Slater*, for example, left the United States for England in early 1944 brimming with a cargo of sulfur. It was a dark night three days into the voyage when another ship in its convoy, the concrete ship *SS Vitruvius*, collided with the *Slater*, opening that gaping hole in the bow. Captain and crew scrambled to adjust the ship's ballast so that it would stay afloat, but the sulfur run was through. The crew aborted that mission and steamed in reverse for the American coast they had just left.[241]

That they reached Bermuda instead was no great disappointment to the young men aboard. Indeed, eighteen-year-old Charles Mitchell, part of the waylaid crew, recalled spending "a good three weeks" in Bermuda, having "a delightful time on bicycles touring the beautiful island while Navy Sea Bees patched the hole in the *Slater*'s bow."[242]

It turns out that one of the many advantages proponents of concrete ships touted—that repair of the vessels was to be far easier and faster than steel hulls—was baloney. The patch the Sea Bees put on its gaping bow was awkward and spotty. The *Slater* was never again seaworthy enough to haul loads of sugar, sulfur, or anything else.[243]

After top brass said it would sail no more, the *Slater*'s mission changed once again, and it entered military service as a training ship, allowing stevedores to learn the ropes before handling genuine cargo where an error would be much costlier. A couple other McCloskey ships served as trainers alongside it. The *Vitruvius*, the ship that rammed and pierced the *Slater*, was sunk with another concrete ship off the coast of Normandy, France, as a breakwater ahead of the D-Day invasion.[244]

As the protracted fight against the Japanese developed into an island-hopping campaign in the Pacific, the concrete ships proved well suited for that theater of war. Among the Allies' many needs there was floating storage space, berths for the clothes, food, and munitions to support the steady advance of Allied forces. Two-thirds of McCloskey's concrete ships served in this capacity. A handful saw some use ferrying cargo in the Pacific after the war, visiting ports like Melbourne, Manila, and Shanghai.[245]

After the war, however, the concrete ships' versatility was no match for the glut of watercraft the war-weary nation had on hand. There were simply too many ships for the finicky concrete vessels to be of any worth. In 1950, McCloskey's two dozen steamers were part of a 2,278-ship fleet that the US government had sitting idly at anchor in ten reserve fleets.[246]

The concrete ships had the added distinction of being oddballs, not to mention ungainly and funny looking. Although there were large-scale efforts to build commercial and recreational vessels out of concrete well into the 1970s, concrete ships never captured a positive vibe, despite a century of evidence showing those craft were, for all intents and purposes, just as safe as any others. The concrete ships seemed destined for some anonymous end, perhaps a sunken reef deep in the ocean.[247]

It turns out, however, that a couple buyers were in the market for, of all things, the type of long and lean rock-solid stability that only concrete freighters could offer.

Virginia's Eastern Shore, the bottom of the Delmarva Peninsula, is a finger of land that arcs gently southward, pointing toward the bustling metropolitan area of Hampton Roads. The gap between these points of land, eleven miles of wide-open water, is the mouth of the Chesapeake Bay. Until 1964, if you wanted to move across this stretch of sea, you had to swim or take a boat. Today there is the modern convenience of the Chesapeake Bay Bridge-Tunnel.

In the late 1940s, the Virginia Ferry Corporation decided to move its northern terminal from the town of Cape Charles seven miles south to a featureless spot on the shoreline called Kiptopeke. What the Virginia Ferry Corporation was gaining in time savings—the new location shaved thirty minutes off the ferry trip, contemporary promotions boasted—they were sacrificing in the sheltered harbor of Cape Charles. To buffet their new terminal against the waves that grew across the width of the bay before crashing into Kiptopeke beach, the Virginia Ferry Corporation purchased nine concrete ships for $270,000, almost $18 million less than the vessels had cost to construct four years earlier.[248]

In 1949, the ferry corporation partially sunk those nine ships, resting on the bottom with their top halves above the surface of the water. In an unnecessary show of machismo, workmen dynamited two of the ships, but realized soon afterward that the simpler and much less dangerous method of simply opening hatches to let water in did just as good a job as blowing big holes in them. That, of course, was not as much fun.[249]

Seven McCloskey ships also went to Powell River, British Columbia, Canada, to serve as a breakwater, but without being sunk. To this day, those vessels still float with relatively little maintenance, vindication for all the cheerleaders who touted concrete's longevity.[250]

The nine concrete ships that showed up at Kiptopeke were still fully rigged, and even though they showed bumps and bruises from their wartime service—fading paint, stained concrete—they nonetheless remained seaworthy down to the day-to-day items that kept crews functioning. The galleys retained fixtures and silverware. There were bunks and navigational equipment still on board, surplus bric-a-brac the US Maritime Commission, still flush with a wartime fleet, were no doubt glad to part with.[251]

The ships excelled at their new calling, although admittedly, a career as a sunken breakwater was not all that challenging. They offered safe harbor and calm seas for captains carrying precious cargo. Nervous ferry crews caught in the Chesapeake's nasty microbursts often looked with relief to the concrete ships, stalwart sentinels in the sea. While commuters might have thanked their lucky stars a time or two for the sunken ships that secured safe passage, mischievous locals liked them, too, because they offered a diversion from the humdrum routines of the agricultural Eastern Shore.

The ferry director, of all people, used the concrete ships as a secluded drinks and poker club that was out of earshot of players' nagging wives. Adventurous youth likewise climbed aboard to explore the ships' quarters, despite that trespassing was forbidden. All the supplementals that arrived with the ships, anything that wasn't tied down and a lot that was, began to make off for homes unknown.[252]

But it wasn't just the fixtures that were lost over time, because the elements never let up, and the burnished facades on these stalwart old veterans began to lose their luster. Slowly, their paint chipped off, and chunks of concrete succumbed to gravity.[253]

There was an effort in the 1990s to revive the concrete ships' memory as part of a proposed resort campground development onshore. The plan called for the construction of an interpretive platform that would allow visitors to motor out to the relics to access a space that looked down on the old hulls. When the financing for the resort fell through, though, so did plans to preserve the nearly forgotten vessels.[254]

The concrete ships are easy enough to see standing onshore from the former terminal where cars once loaded up for the hour-and-a-quarter-long trip south. A decent pair of binoculars gives curious landlubbers a feel for the toll that time has exacted from these hulks.[255]

But it is in the shadow of these leviathans that their decay is most palpable. Their concrete is textured, stained, feeble. They have not aged well. A couple of the holds are blown wide open, and it's possible to slip a small craft inside. Slapping waves echo ghostlike in the chambers. A ladder from the deck above descends deep into the water. This hold might have contained sugar from Cuba or sulfur bound for England or clothing or fuel that American servicemen used to fight the Pacific Theater's bloodiest battles.

The ships' sad appearance belies the fact that they're still very much of use five decades after they sank because from the moment they went down, they became something that's hard to come by in that relatively featureless stretch of the Chesapeake Bay's floor: habitat.

The ships instantly became, to the local ecosystem anyway, hundreds of thousands of square feet of vertical structure above the stifling silt they now rest atop. Below surface, oysters and barnacles quickly latched on to the concrete, a near-perfect substrate to take advantage of the tidewater that always flushes new plankton by. At low tide, the ships appear to emit an audible hiss as these creatures filter water. The old vessels are craggy, gnarled, passaged places to hide and ambush prey. Blue crabs wait expectantly for what's left of anything larger predators didn't eat whole. Larger fish troll the ships for easy pickings. Fisherman troll the ships for larger fish.

On deck, shoreline plants have taken root, tall grasses uniformly curved in one direction thanks to the prevailing winds that blow toward shore. Shorebirds long ago found the concrete ships a suitable home relatively free from human intrusion. Pelicans shelter in the quarters where crewmen once sweated through torrid Pacific nights. Seagulls perch on the poop deck squawking their annoyance at the odd fisherman who comes a bit too close. It's their guano that's made these once-barren decks spring to life.

Today the stern of the *Slater* has been torn wide open by decades of exposure, and boaters can see clear into the sleeping quarters where men contributing to the war effort once slept. Those failing walls illuminate that important slice of their life, of all merchant mariners' lives, and shed light, too, on what's left of a forgotten war effort and all the life that moved in when so many others cast them aside.

Chapter 12

Nike Missile Batteries: Annihilation Beneath Suburban Streets

By a conservative estimate, there was once enough firepower under a field in Wayland, Massachusetts, to fill a freight train three and a half miles long with dynamite. Standing beside that secluded meadow today, it's hard to imagine the scale of potential destruction that once sat a few feet below the surface. Dainty wildflowers sway in a soft breeze, bobbing as bees bounce among them, gathering pollen. A stand of mature timber surrounds the meadow, and pine boughs reach low as if they want to shake your hand.[256]

You might be fooled into believing this is some isolated mountain lea were it not for the rolling hum of traffic not too far in the distance. Wayland is a quaint suburb fifteen miles west of Boston. Suburbia spilled into this countryside decades ago, but the town never strayed far from its rural roots. Here, winding roads weave through a charming tapestry of stone walls and old churches. In the 1950s, this landscape fit a particular set of criteria the US government had for an important project. It was not in too many residential backyards, yet still within firing range of a city that policymakers surmised the Soviet Union would love nothing more than to blow to smithereens.[257]

The meadow in Wayland is part of what's left of B-73, one small piece of a military program responsible for protecting the nation's major cities from nuclear holocaust. In the first years of the Cold War, when fear and uncertainty gripped Americans, the US government planned for a worst-case scenario: Soviet bombers armed with nuclear weapons dropping their payloads on big American cities. The government erected a few barriers to make that mode of attack as difficult as possible.

B-73 was one of them. There were 274 others just like it, most arranged in neat rings around more than three dozen American cities and military bases. These batteries made up a chapter of Cold War history that's largely fading from American memory: the Nike air defense missile system.[258]

The Nike program served the nation admirably for two and a half decades, but when its time had ended, the scoresheet wasn't as impressive as other military endeavors. Nike shot down no enemy planes, made no combat veterans. Oddly enough, that was a measure of success; Nike, by its existence, helped secure American lives and property, keeping a sort of begrudging peace between two warring nations through Mutual Assured Destruction, the idea that war would result in both their annihilation.

Now, almost all Nike batteries have been obscured by time. Some, like B-73, have made the unlikely transition from bricks and mortar to teeming pasture. Most have not. They're in various stages of decay, with no hope of salvation, much less interpretation, for those that are too far gone. That sort of preservation is a pipe dream anyway.

Money is tight and Mother Nature is pitiless. Saving just a small piece of a single Nike battery is a herculean task. Attempts to save local Nike sites have begun with promise only to crash soon afterward. But it turns out there's a next best option to keep Nike missile batteries—not to mention our other forsaken footprints—in public memory, despite all the forces conspiring to wipe them off the map.

Nearly two hundred miles southwest of Wayland, I arrived on a perfect summer day at the Sandy Hook Unit of the Gateway National Recreation Area. Sandy Hook, New Jersey, is an arcing finger of land that points north from the mainland into New York Harbor. Unlike the hordes of beach bunnies coming to Sandy Hook that day, I wasn't there for the sand and surf.

Sandy Hook, location of the now-decommissioned Fort Hancock and owned by the National Park Service, was vital to America's coastal defense beginning in the nineteenth century. When the time came to choose the sites for the nineteen Nike missile batteries to defend New York City, this spit was a no-brainer. It was close to the city but not too close, and it was government-owned and right up against the Atlantic Ocean.[259]

NY-56, as this battery was known, guarded New York from 1955 to 1974. With the closing of the Nike program, NY-56 was shuttered and well on its way to decay like the hundreds of others around the country; scrubby and succulent vegetation that thrives so well at Sandy Hook soon choked out the structures. Corrosive saltwater ate at the battery built on that sea-soaked ecosystem. An inglorious end for a program that protected the nation admirably for two decades.[260]

When I arrived at NY-56, I found it a stretch to imagine that this was the nerve center of a weapons system sophisticated enough to eliminate enemy airplanes too far away to see. The site was surrounded by an eight-foot chain-link fence so rusty it seemed like you could get lockjaw from just looking at it. A paved and well-traveled bike path kissed a corner near the entrance. Most of the bathing-suited bikers paid no mind to ominous towers that loomed on the other side.

There to greet me at the gate was Bill Jackson, a Nike veteran with the square demeanor and diction of a man for whom the Army's rhythms took and stuck. Jackson served at NY-56 while it was operational and proudly wears a decorated hat that says as much. As Jackson swung back the gate, a biker slowed on the path and asked him for directions to the nearest beach. Emotionless, he gave precise directions—no more, no less.

He turned back toward me. "I'm glad you're here but I apologize that I have to run off to a meeting. We're trying to acquire a piece of equipment for the site and, unfortunately, we have to work around other people's schedules. There's another gentleman who will be happy to give you a tour."

That was Pete DeMarco. Tall and stocky with a white mustache to match his hair, DeMarco had been volunteering at this site for ten years, but his journey here began decades ago as a young man. "I knew I was going to be drafted, so I signed up to avoid that," DeMarco told me. "The recruiter said I could be a fire distribution controller. It sounded exciting, and I thought, 'Why not?' They gave me my dream sheet asking where I wanted to go. I put Florida and ended up working with Nikes in Alaska. I learned a lot about the Army at that point."

After he left the Army, DeMarco had a long career in air traffic control and later, when National Park Service officials began tours of NY-56 in the early 2000s, DeMarco was eager to look over this site, only a couple hours' drive from his home on Long Island. He eventually stepped into the role of vice president of the Fort Hancock Nike Association.

DeMarco became part of a group of committed volunteers that have achieved something uncommon: the preservation of a Nike missile site. Only three other batteries in the entire country—near San Francisco, Anchorage, and in the Florida Everglades—are in any condition to permit tours. Hundreds of others languish in suburban America. Nike batteries ring a dozen major East Coast cities from Boston to Miami, along with Midwestern and Pacific Coast metropolitan areas.[261]

In addition to being cleared of the vegetation that has choked so many other Nike sites, NY-56 has largely been restored with components that the Fort Hancock Nike Association has bought and begged from other sites around the world.

DeMarco explained that each Nike missile battery had two operational areas. The first, where we were talking, was called the Integrated Fire Control area, and this was usually combined with an administrative center where soldiers slept, ate, and carried out administrative duties. A half-dozen radar domes on elevated platforms blanketed the sky night and day searching for incoming enemy aircraft. The domes have long since been removed, the lonesome towers now bleeding rust like tears.[262]

The nerve center of NY-56 was a somewhat ramshackle looking hut called the battery control trailer. Two wings resembling modified shipping containers branched off a central connecting corridor, the interior of which had been meticulously restored to recreate the areas where operators could receive and interpret data and act if necessary. One trailer was devoted to identifying targets based on radar readings. On the opposite end of the central corridor was a space where a commander could use a missile guidance system to direct missile launches. In both wings of this restored command post, flat banks of round radar screens and analog switches give the setup a decided tech-retro feel. "I've had college-age computer techs in here before, and they all marvel at this stuff," DeMarco said. "They've never seen it before."[263]

Outside, a couple administrative and other support structures completed the part of NY-56 that was fit for public tours, including a generator building and what appeared to be an equipment shed.[264]

All these motley structures formed an irregular courtyard of sorts, and in the center of it all was a Nike Hercules missile, deactivated and inert. Beside it on the ground, another was wedged tight in a metal tube. "We haven't figured out how to get it out yet," DeMarco said.

These missiles—forty-one feet long and nearly three feet in diameter with several sets of fins—capable of intercepting enemy targets at an altitude of one hundred thousand feet, were the second version of the Nike. The first, called Nike Ajax, were likewise supersonic, but they contained conventional explosives. Hercules upped the ante. "With a conventional warhead you have to hit an aircraft almost directly," DeMarco said. "With a nuke, you put it in the area, and it turns the whole squadron to sand."[265]

The few structures DeMarco showed me were only one small part of the complex that would have made that possible. He invited me to follow him down a dirt and sand road that descends into the tall weeds and mature trees that surround these preserved remnants of NY-56. The tour he normally gives visitors doesn't follow this route, but he wanted to give me an idea of what the small display out front had been reclaimed from.

Almost every inch of ground had some manner of wild growth, such as gnarled, knotty pines and phragmites reeds twice my height, red cedar, sumac, and all manner of grasses. And remarkably, amid this tangle, almost as if it was an afterthought, stood all the other manmade fabric that once served basic human needs: barracks fashioned of corrugated metal, a leaning basketball goal, a forlorn phone booth. I asked DeMarco if there would be any effort to clear this growth. "Probably not," he said. "It's all we can do just to keep up with what we have out front."[266]

"Was nature the biggest stumbling block?" I wondered.

"That and money," DeMarco explained. "A single can of paint remover for aviation-grade paint that we need to refurbish the missiles is a hundred bucks. As nice as it would be to restore this whole site or to bring back some of the others around the country, money isn't going to magically appear to make that possible."

Underscoring what a tall order maintaining one small piece of a Nike battery is, DeMarco and I headed to the other primary component of this and all other 274 like them: a separate area consisting of an underground magazine and launchpad, where soldiers armed and deployed the Ajax and, later, Hercules missiles. At Sandy Hook, the launchpad is a mile south of the Integrated Fire Control area, but likewise surrounded by a fence and usually off limits to tour groups. There are just far too many ways people could hurt themselves there, and DeMarco and other volunteers concentrated their efforts at the less dangerous of the two sites.

The flat concrete pad was peppered with hatches and blast plates, caked with rust and seized shut because of the saltwater blowing in from the Atlantic. The elevator that once raised Nikes in and out of the magazine is stuck in the down position. A jury-rigged plywood cover keeps out rain. DeMarco managed to find a small hatch with some promise and heaved it open. A rebar ladder descended into a chamber which presumably led to a labyrinth of passages. It was hard to tell because I only got a four-foot by four-foot glimpse looking down the hatch.[267]

DeMarco shut the portal then looked down and closed his eyes. "There was a hallway here," he said, shuffling along on the concrete, marking off the layout below him. It was forty years later, but he remembered as if he was there yesterday. "You went four feet and then came to a blast proof door, right . . . here," he said, turning left to enter a room eight feet below him. Had I not interrupted his train of thought by commending him on his remarkable memory, he would've eventually come to the place where the missiles were stored.

With soldiers working together at both the Integrated Fire Control area and the launchpad, NY-56 could identify and shoot down a squadron of enemy planes with surprising speed. In late 1958, Army officials required that twenty-five percent of Nike batteries be prepared to deploy a missile within five minutes.[268]

Despite that state of hyper-readiness, improved technology made the Nike air defense missile system obsolete. By the 1960s, the Americans and Soviets employed a different delivery system for nuclear weaponry: the intercontinental ballistic missile. The Nike system was powerless against this new threat, and while some batteries remained active well beyond this development, nearly all of them were shuttered by 1975, and two decades of Nike air defense came to an end.[269]

There may have been a sort of mystique about Nike batteries because they were officially top secret and off limits, but thanks to aggressive PR campaigns by the military, neighbors more or less knew what was inside the perimeter. When the Nike program ended, communities regarded those batteries as outdated military bric-a-brac, even though they were the largest domestic peacetime deployment of military matériel.[270]

It helps to think of the context, too. In the mid-1970s, the United States had just slogged through the end of a costly and unpopular war, a corruption scandal that resulted in the unprecedented resignation of the president, and a new paradigm in civil rights. In the midst of all this upheaval, the closing of Nike missile batteries garnered little notice, much less any effort to keep any of them around for posterity.

That's not to say that the sites weren't well-loved during their active years. The small, isolated enclaves were impeccably maintained, if for no other reason than military discipline demanded it. But there was something else, too, among Nike service members—a pride of service, and of the expertise necessary to make Nike batteries run well.

A newsletter, the *ARADCOM Argus*, showcased notable goings-on within the Nike community. There were even beauty pageants to name "Miss Nike" from surrounding neighborhoods. Soldiers cultivated an esprit de corps strong enough to spawn message boards and reunion groups four decades later. "I had a group of vets from Alaska in here, and I saw tears in some eyes," DeMarco said. "Many of these guys haven't seen a setup like this in forty years."[271]

Even that sentimentality couldn't save Nike batteries, though. They weren't as conspicuous as the hot wars of the Cold War's adolescence. There were no front lines, no medals for valor under enemy fire. Nike never had to be deployed in combat. Apathy carried over when the Cold War became history. Relatively little is written in modern history books about the role of the Nike program compared to higher profile events.

The military held onto decommissioned Nike batteries, but maintaining them was not a high priority, so they were at the mercy of nature. Without regular maintenance to keep brush at bay, land that had once been closely cropped went through natural succession. Local flora and fauna flourished. Because many of the magazines were under the concrete launchpads, and thus well below ground, they soon filled up with water. All those subterranean corridors and storage areas have been filled with water for decades.[272]

That's one feature that makes NY-56 unique. Its magazine is bone dry. That's because it's a stone's throw from the Atlantic Ocean. "You dig down inches, you're at the water table," DeMarco said. "This is one of few sites where they put the magazine on top of the ground and built up the terrain around it."

For the support buildings, nature's reclamation wasn't all that difficult. This was military-issue construction, built not for comfort, but for function. Although the underground magazines were supposed to be blast proof, the simple structures above ground were anything but. Cinderblocks and corrugated metal and timber framing were the preferred material, and those were especially vulnerable to decay. The masonry crumbled as vines crept over them. Nature made quick work of the roofs and windows and the deterioration snowballed from there.

From the edge of the launchpad, DeMarco pointed out to the rolling Atlantic a hundred yards or so out. "That used to be much farther away," he said. "Sandy Hook naturally migrates north. The hook is getting bigger at the expense of this shoreline." He looked down at his feet, at the edge of the launchpad. "It's only a matter of time."

Healthy nor'easters and tropical storms, as with Hurricane Sandy in October 2012, accelerate the decay. At NY-56's Integrated Fire Control area, DeMarco showed me a line of tape a couple feet up the side of the cinderblock facade of a building that shows how high the water came during Hurricane Sandy. In another nearby structure, he pointed to patches of sky where eaves should be, taken by merciless winds. Over near the launchpad at the old warhead building, then being used by volunteers to restore an old missile, the storm surge rushed through, knocking out panels of the rolling garage door and scattering the fins of the missile hundreds of yards away. They never found one of them. Preserving and interpreting that one small portion of that one small Nike site is now the battle these vets fight.[273]

The Fort Hancock Nike Association is lucky that this site happens to fall within the boundaries of popular federal property; some 9.2 million people visit Gateway National Recreation Area annually, and while the old Nike site captures only a small fraction of those visitors, the NPS nevertheless offers what meager help it can in terms of resources, such as paint, which goes a long way toward keeping NY-56 afloat. DeMarco conceded that the government bureaucracy often proceeds at a snail's pace, but proceed it does.[274]

That's more than can be said for scores of other Nike sites the US government gave to local municipalities or simply let sit as part of their inventory of surplus land, overgrown and forgotten. All that lost history may rub some people the wrong way, but it's unrealistic to expect that any great number will be folded into the historic properties that communities cherish. There are too many of them, for one. And that's to say nothing of the enormous effort this would take, which would leave preservationists swamped and coffers spent.

But it turns out that there's a good alternative to the unrealistic goal of trying to preserve the physical remnants of Nike cast across the landscape, and the kernel of inspiration for that effort leads back to that pretty meadow in Wayland, Massachusetts.

Among the first items that jumped out at me in Dave Tewksbury's well-stocked office at Hamilton College in Clinton, New York, were a couple small boxes containing Renwal Blueprint Models. The kit? Nike with Launcher and Crew. I'd seen plenty of vehicles, tanks, and aircraft models, but Nike missiles? Who would have thought? "Found those online," he told me. "I couldn't pass them up."[275]

Tewksbury found a lot more than Nike models online, and his work attracted praise from preservationists and vets who lament the reality that little can be done for the abandoned Nike missile batteries that pepper the landscape. Tewksbury was a GIS specialist for Hamilton's Geosciences Department until his retirement several years ago. He was a computer guy who supported instruction and research with all the mapping and imagery tools such a tech-heavy discipline demands. Tewksbury is in his sixties with a beard that's more salt than pepper and an earnest stare that's almost penetrating. He's a wealth of information, and what he doesn't know offhand he can find among the scores of binders and reference books, not to mention the half-dozen monitors, packed into his office lair.

Long before he found his way up the hill at Hamilton, Tewksbury was a boy in Wayland. He grew up a stone's throw from B-73. "What's strange is that I didn't even know it until a few years ago," he said. Not until he saw a local high school history project posted online did Tewksbury realize there had been a Nike battery in his backyard. "I began to wonder if there were others."

And boy were there. He found a strong Nike presence online, including a zoomable map of Nike missile batteries. Tewksbury was not the first person to muse on the fate of those hundreds of forgotten sites. He did, however, bring a unique set of expertise and tools along with his curiosity.[276]

So he began peeling back layers on B-73, gathering historic photographs of the site, all of which were publicly accessible and available with a little digging. He found historic aerial photographs of the Wayland battery near his boyhood home dating to 1957 (when it was an active Nike battery), 1995, 2001, 2003, and 2010. It was like a flip book of nature's reclamation of the site.

And while he was looking at his old neighbor from above, he drew on another aerial image, too: lidar. Light Detection and Ranging is a method of remote sensing to identify surface features. Airplanes sporting specialized lidar equipment can precisely map contours of the earth within inches by measuring the data collected from pulsing lasers. What results is an image with all the extraneous layers, such as structures and trees, peeled back, resulting in a 3D image of the ground reminiscent of those airport body scans.

So Tewksbury pulled up the lidar scan of B-73's launching area and found a curious feature: "These sites all have a distinct pattern on the ground and that makes it easy to look for them. It's a road through an earthen berm that was used to arm missiles," he explained. This is a feature as common to every Nike launch area as concrete and cinderblocks. Just in case an inadvertent explosion occurred while soldiers armed the missiles, this feature directed the blast upward where it was less likely to damage adjacent buildings.[277]

It also armed Tewksbury with a telltale signature to look for, because once he had gathered all the visual data on the Wayland site, he began looking for more, and it wasn't always easy. For instance, the maps online weren't always correct. Often the tags indicating an old Nike battery were dead on, but other times just dead wrong.

What's more, development has often obliterated any trace of many Nike sites' former life, that telltale berm included. Those rural lands so well suited for unobtrusive missile batteries have, in the forty-plus years since their demise, been blanketed by suburban growth.

I peeked over Tewksbury's shoulder as he brought up a historic black-and-white aerial image of the launchpad of PH-67, one of a dozen batteries around Philadelphia. When the military constructed PH-67 in the mid-1950s, Upper Chichester, Pennsylvania was a patchwork of farm plots within walking distance of the Delaware border. Not so anymore.

Tewksbury used software to overlay a modern aerial shot exactly over the historic one. In place of the flat launchpad and adjacent berm, the bright red roof and baseball fields of a sprawling complex that turned out to be Hilltop Elementary School.

"I see this all the time," he said. "They turn into schools, housing developments, parks, even prisons. There's even a launching area in Virginia that a McMansion is built right on top of. I'd love to find out if they know what's underneath their house."

For instance, the town of Wayland, when it acquired B-73 in 2004, permitted developers to create a sixteen-unit affordable townhome community. Construction crews filled in the underground chambers, put soil on the old launchpad, planted native flowers as green space adjacent to the neighborhood, and called the new park Oxbow Meadows. Walking paths snaked around the property. The berm where soldiers armed Nike missiles is covered in trees. In the late 2010s, town officials approved construction of a playing field on the ground, a plan that many neighbors opposed because of it would disrupt the tranquil meadow the site had become. The town eventually won out. The site, in recent years, has been converted into a soccer field.[278]

There are few visible traces of B-73's Integrated Fire Control area a couple miles east. Now it's Drumlin Farm, a wildlife sanctuary and camp owned by Mass Audubon. Of all days I happened to visit to look for any remnants of the Nike site, it turned out to be summer camp drop-off day. I poked around some, but a lone stranger, disheveled and unshaven from several days' travel, slinking around and shooting photos here and there, garnered numerous scowls from parents dropping off their kids, so I beat a hasty retreat. But it didn't matter; the Cold War had left Drumlin Farm long ago.

Just as common are Nike sites that have seen no reuse other than nature's reclamation, where what's left gives a good snapshot of what things might look like were people to suddenly vanish from the Earth. They are nameless and forgotten, now eyesores tucked in corners of communities where few folks venture.

Whatever their present state, Tewksbury showed a way to ensure their memory using the digital tools at his disposal. "Regardless of what happens to a site, we can say something about it. Even if it's been bulldozed or paved over, we have other resources that can tell a story about each place."

And as technology advances, that's a way to keep history alive, even when time and progress erase the physical traces. The past can peek through its destruction and speak to us through the technology that defines our modern lives.

As for the Nike missile sites, Tewksbury envisions a geo-referenced database that allows anyone to research the batteries using common mapping software. Click on a missile site and it will bring up historic photos, archival data such as old pictures, news clippings, or recollections.

"I view this as a work in progress. As more technology and resources become available, those are more pieces that can be tied into this puzzle," he said. "Computerized mapping has revolutionized understanding. That's the only way most of these places are going to survive."

Conclusion

History is Not Abandoned if You Find It

Near my home in James City County, Virginia, is a remote property containing ragged busts of all forty-three United States presidents through George W. Bush. The heads, most about eighteen feet high, are in a sad state of disrepair, their concrete cracked and crumbling, rebar exposed and rusting. Layers of Woodrow Wilson's face are flaking off, making a grotesque zombie of the twenty-eighth president. A hole yawns in the back of Abe Lincoln's head as if some giant John Wilkes Booth had put it there himself.

The spectacle is the result of a failed tourist attraction called Presidents Park that I first became aware of when I wrote about its closure for a magazine in 2012. The park's backers had grand visions for the attraction, but tourists didn't share that enthusiasm. After the park's foreclosure, the busts went to live on a private farm. Investors hoped to sell them off piecemeal, but it turns out there wasn't much demand for the larger-than-life heads of Millard Fillmore and Chester Arthur.

The idea of presidential busts rotting away to oblivion in the middle of a secluded field was so captivating that major media outlets—among them NBC, *National Geographic,* and *Smithsonian* magazine—picked up the story. Drone enthusiasts flew clandestine reconnaissance missions over the heads.

The owner restricts access because he doesn't want interlopers poking around; it is a working property with heavy equipment and few safeguards for pedestrians. I had occasion to visit the heads when the family acting as caretakers of the property invited my son, a classmate of their daughter, to a birthday party. In between splashes in the kiddie pool and whacks of the piñata, the other parents and I wandered through the silent heads, fascinated and speechless.

Although the run of Presidents Park was not particularly long and the idea of it unique but not particularly historic, its arc serves to drive home a point: people are constantly making and abandoning history. Like those heads, most history won't survive. Nor should it. The amount of time and resources we would have to devote to preserve and interpret even a small fraction of important events and places would quickly bankrupt public coffers, divert man hours from other necessary goals, and devalue truly historic sites by flooding the market with too much cultural static.

But we can get creative to save what we value. Technology, for one thing, will play a part, whether it's physical maps of earthworks or teasing the contours from forgotten Nike missile batteries using lidar. Public buy-in is a critical component, too, as with the Abandoned Pennsylvania Turnpike. Federal and state protection is ideal, but commercialization can also be part of the toolkit, as Georgia's Consolidated Gold Mine demonstrates. Despite our best efforts, though, some history, like Kiptopeke's concrete ships and further offshore, Watts Island, will succumb to the forces of time and nature, and slip from our grasp entirely.

But personal interactions with forgotten historic and cultural sites must be part of the calculus. I've tried since the beginning of my journalistic career to find, acknowledge, and, when possible, seek out and share the story of abandoned history—at least that within easy reach of me. That counts for something. And my hope with this project is that readers, too, will find their own abandoned history and make their own experiences. At least the crowds will be smaller, or nonexistent.

There were numerous places I visited during the course of my research that never made it into this book. There were even a couple chapters I wrote that I ended up culling before putting this to bed. What's more, I never made it much beyond the East Coast for this project, having plenty to choose from within easy reach of the Eastern Seaboard. Abandoned history is ubiquitous.

I drove and walked over rutted country roads in search of American Indian burial mounds that nature washed away or, more often, that nineteenth and early twentieth century looters destroyed for souvenirs (or contemporary "research," which often involved the site's destruction). I circled aging city blocks in search of property where people once hoped they would find utopia, a perfect and closed society where they could shut out the rest of the damnable world. I even sought out ancient, geologic history that no human being ever took part in, and stood beneath Daggett Rock, a house-sized boulder that a glacier deposited far away from its point of origin many millennia ago.

And that's to say nothing of the numerous places I visited and wrote briefly about for this project's companion blog, Abandoned Country, and for a yearlong series on Virginia's disappearing history in *Distinction* magazine. I sat on masonry that once made up the public facade of the United States Capitol, now stacked ingloriously in a wooded Washington, DC, park. On Jamestown Island, the site of America's first permanent English settlement, archaeologists told me of an impending crisis, how rising seas were forcing them to do the unthinkable: remove archaeological artifacts from the ground without proper documentation before the encroaching, brackish water destroyed them forever. I watched as Virginia-born oyster shuckers worked, the last of a dying breed, their labor increasingly replaced by foreign, itinerant workers.

I encourage you to find your own abandoned history.

In all the places I visited for this project I tried to put myself in the place of the people central to these stories. Wherever I stood, whatever I saw, whatever I sensed, I was aware that I was looking at meaningful work—contributing to a war effort, feeding a family, or simply putting a personal touch on a lasting endeavor. The least we can do—and in most places, the only thing we can do—is seek out and acknowledge the people who went about their lives, making us who we are today.

Endnotes

INTRODUCTION

1 Robert H. Burgess, "The Schooner William T. Parker, A Profile in Miniature" *The Chesapeake Skipper* (April 1949), 19, 33. Robert H. Burgess, *Chesapeake Sailing Craft; Recollections of Robert H. Burgess, Expanded Edition* (Centreville, MD: Tidewater Publishers, 2005), 83, 290. Cecil S. Bragg, *Ocracoke Island: Pearl of the Outer Banks* (Manteo, NC: Times Printing Company, 1973), 162-163. Wilse Jackson talks about lumber piled nine feet high on the deck of the Parker.

2 Bragg, 161.

3 Will Englund, "Chesapeake Bay is a Graveyard of Many a Ship Over Centuries," *The Baltimore Sun*, October 14, 1995. Bragg, 159-161.

4 In *Chesapeake Sailing Craft*, Burgess mentions groundings or capsizing three times: August 1899, September 1908 and 1915. Contemporary newspapers account for at least two others. See *The Norfolk Virginian*, November 7, 1896, p. 7, and *The Times Dispatch*, March 18, 1911, p. 1.

5 Bragg, 166.

6 Burgess, "The Schooner William T. Parker, A Profile in Miniature," 19. Burgess, *Chesapeake Sailing Craft*, 292. Burgess reports that the ship that collided with the Parker was the Commercial Bostonian.

CHAPTER 1

7 Woodrow Borah, "Chapter 1: The Historical Demography of Aboriginal and Colonial America: An Attempt at Perspective," in *The Native Populations of the Americas in 1492, Second Edition*, ed. William M. Deneven (Madison, Wisconsin: The University of Wisconsin Press, 1992), 13-34.

8 John H Hann. A History of the Timucua Indians and Missions (Gainesville, Florida: University Press of Florida, 1996).

9 Emma Marris, *Rambunctious Garden; Saving Nature in a Post-Wild World* (New York: Bloomsbury, 2011), Chapter 3, "The Forest Primeval."

10 Murray Carpenter, "Native American Secrets Lie Buried in Huge Shell Mounds," *The New York Times* (New York, NY), October 19, 2017, accessed February 20, 2022, https://www.nytimes.com/2017/10/19/science/native-americans-shell-middens-maine.html?_r=0

11 About the extinction of the passenger pigeon, see Joel Greenburg, *A Feathered River Across the Sky* (Bloomsbury: New York, 2014).

12 See the publication "Kingsley Plantation" from Timucuan Ecological and Historical Preserve, National Park Service, accessed February 20, 2022. https://www.nps.gov/timu/learn/historyculture/kp_tabby.htm

13 Carpenter, "Native American Secrets Lie Buried in Huge Shell Mounds," accessed February 20, 2022. "Whaleback Shell Midden," *Maine Bureau of Parks and Lands*, Maine.gov, 2013. http://www.maine.gov/dacf/parks/discover_history_explore_nature/history/whaleback/index.shtml

14 "Whaleback Shell Midden," Maine.gov. David Sanger and Mary Jo Elson Sanger, "Boom and Bust on the River: The story of the Damariscotta Oyster Shell Heaps," *Archaeology of Eastern North America*, Vol. 14 (Fall 1986), 65-78. David Sanger and Mary Jo Elson Sanger, "The Damariscotta Oyster Shell Heaps," *Northeastern Naturalist,* Vol. 4, No. 2 (1997), 93-102.

15 "Whaleback Shell Midden," Maine.gov.

16 "Sea Level Rise and the Damariscotta River Oyster Shell Middens," Maine Geological Survey, April 2011. "Whaleback Shell Midden," Maine.gov.

17 Sanger and Sanger, "Boom and Bust on the River," 68. "Maine Midden Minders," The University of Maine, accessed February 20, 2022, https://umaine.edu/middenminders/.

18 "Land Areas, Inland-Water Areas, and Lengths of Shorelines of Maryland's Counties," *Maryland Geological Survey*, Maryland Department of Natural Resources, accessed February 20, 2022. http://www.mgs.md.gov/geology/areas_and_lengths.html. Lara Lutz, "Middens Offer Pearls of Wisdom about Chesapeake's Geology," *Bay Journal*, October 2011. https://www.bayjournal.com/news/people/middens-offer-pearls-of-wisdom-about-chesapeakes-geology/article_c7670365-7949-5b50-911c-d7f952276a89.html. Rick C. Torbin, Gregory Henkes and John S. Wah, "A Late Holocene Radiocarbon Chronology for the Shell Middens of Fishing Bay, Maryland," *Archaeology of Eastern North America*, Vol. 39 (2011), 153-167.

19 *Chesapeake Quarterly* and *Bay Journal*, "Come High Water; Sea Level Rise and Chesapeake Bay. A Special Report from *Chesapeake Quarterly* and *Bay Journal*," College Park, MD: Maryland Sea Grant, 2015, 6-10. http://www.mdsg.umd.edu/sites/default/files/files/Come%20High%20Water-Report-2015.pdf. Jack Eggleston and Jason Pope, "Land Subsidence and Relative Sea-Level Rise in the Southern Chesapeake Bay Region," U.S. Department of the Interior Circular 1392, Reston, Virginia: U.S. Geological Survey, 2013, 14. https://pubs.usgs.gov/circ/1392/pdf/circ1392.pdf.

20 Eggleston and Pope, "Land Subsidence and Relative Sea-Level Rise in the Southern Chesapeake Bay Region," 11-12.

21 Virginia Institute of Marine Science, "Recurrent Flooding Study for Tidewater Virginia," January 2013, 111. http://ccrm.vims.edu/recurrent_flooding/Recurrent_Flooding_Study_web.pdf

22 "Come High Water," 4.
23 "Launching from a Sandbar," *NASA Earth Observatory*, National Aeronautics and Space Administration, accessed February 20, 2022. https://earthobservatory.nasa.gov/Features/NASASeaLevel/page3.php
24 "Launching from a Sandbar," accessed December 1, 2019.
25 Jennifer Manis, "Assessing the Effectiveness of Living Shoreline Restoration and Quantifying Wave Attenuation in Mosquito Lagoon, Florida" (2013). Electronic Theses and Dissertations, 2004-2019. 2814, p. 22022. https://stars.library.ucf.edu/etd/2814

CHAPTER 2

26 Otis E. Young, "The Southern Gold Rush, 1828-1836" *The Journal of Southern History*, Vol. 48, No. 3 (August 1982). 375-376.
27 Ibid. 376.
28 David Williams, *The Georgia Gold Rush: Twenty-Niners, Cherokees and Gold Fever*, (Columbia, S.C.: University of South Carolina Press, 1993). 21-22. Drew A. Swanson, *Beyond the Mountains; Commodifying Appalachian Environments* (Athens, GA: University of Georgia Press, 2018), 55-56.
29 Williams, 71.
30 Swanson, 58.
31 Williams, 67-68; Swanson, 58.
32 Wilbur Colvin, "Gold Mining in Georgia," *Scientific American*, July 7, 1900, p. 10. This has contemporary photographs showing the complexity and extent of gold mining equipment. Williams, 73; Young, 378.
33 "Letters from the Alleghany [sic] Mountains; Editors' Correspondence," Author not named. *Weekly National Intelligencer* (Washington, DC), May 6, 1848.
34 "William L. Gwyn to Col. Hamilton Brown, Wilkesboro, N. C. Forsyth, Ga. Jan. 31, 1833" in LETTERS CONCERNING GEORGIA GOLD MINES, 1830-1834. *The Georgia Historical Quarterly*, Vol. 44, No. 3 (September 1960), 343. Swanson, 56-57.
35 Lisa M. Russell *Lost Towns of North Georgia* (Mount Pleasant, S.C.: Arcadia Publishing; The History Press, 2016), "Auraria."; E. Merton Coulter, *Auraria; The Story of a Georgia Gold Mining Town* (Athens, GA: University of Georgia Press, 1955), 8-9. Williams, 59.
36 Young, 384.
37 Fletcher M. Green, "Georgia's Forgotten Industry: Gold Mining; Part II," *The Georgia Historical Quarterly*, Vol. 19, No. 3 (September 1935), 211-212; Young, 385-386.
38 "William L. Gwyn to Col. Hamilton Brown, Wilkesboro, N. C. Forsyth, Ga. Jan. 31, 1833", 343.

39 Green, 212. See also John C. Inscoe, "The 'Ferocious Character' of Antebellum Georgia's Gold Country," Chapter 4 in *Blood in the Hills: A History of Violence in Appalachia*, Bruce E. Stewart, editor. (Lexington, KY: The University Press of Kentucky, 2011), 99-124.
40 Russell, *Lost Towns of North Georgia.*
41 Russell, *Lost Towns of North Georgia.*
42 Russell, *Lost Towns of North Georgia.*
43 W.S. Yeates, "A Preliminary Report on a Part of the Gold Deposits of Georgia," Geological Survey of Georgia, 1896, 48. Also, the interpretive signs at Smithgall Woods State Park on the Martin's Mine Trail contain an immense amount of explanatory information.
44 Personal visit to Chesapeake & Ohio Canal National Historical Park. Information available online: https://www.nps.gov/choh/index.htm.
45 Personal visit to Gold Mining Camp Museum at Monroe Park. Information available: https://www.fauquiercounty.gov/government/departments-h-z/parks-and-recreation/parks/gold-mining-camp-museum
46 "Gold Data Sheet," Mineral Commodity Summaries 2020, United States Geological Survey, 2020. https://pubs.usgs.gov/periodicals/mcs2020/mcs2020-gold.pdf.
47 "History," Consolidated Gold Mine, accessed February 20, 2022. https://consolidatedgoldmine.com/history/ and personal conversation with Parker.
48 "History," Consolidated Gold Mine website.
49 "Mining Operation," Gold N. Gem Grubbin, accessed February 20, 2022. https://goldngemgrubbin.com/mining-operation.
50 Young, 385.
51 "Trail of Tears," Museum of the Cherokee Indian, accessed February 20, 2022. https://mci.org/archives/era/trail-of-tears.
52 "Eastern Band of Cherokee Indians in North Carolina," National Congress of American Indians, accessed February 20, 2022. http://www.ncai.org/tribal-vawa/sdvcj-today/eastern-band-of-cherokee-indians-in-north-carolina.
53 "Hotel" Harrah's Cherokee Casino Resort, accessed February 20, 2022. https://www.caesars.com/harrahs-cherokee.
54 The Eastern Band of Cherokee Indians Treasury department's Office of Budget & Finance publicly announces the amount of the semi-annual per capita payments on their Facebook page. https://www.facebook.com/EBCI-Treasury-Office-of-Budget-Finance-262756020795443/?ref=page_internal. For an exploration of the effects that the per capita payments have on the nation, see Issie Lapowsky, "Free Money: The Surprising Effects of a Basic Income

Supplied by the Government," *Wired*, November 12, 2017, accessed February 20, 2022. https://www.wired.com/story/free-money-the-surprising-effects-of-a-basic-income-supplied-by-government/.

CHAPTER 3

55 Several good sources provide accounts of the circumstances of General Walker's wounding and recovery: Luther S. Dickey, *History of the Eighty-fifty regiment Pennsylvania volunteer infantry, 1861-1865, comprising an authentic narrative of Casey's division at the Battle of Seven Pines* (New York: J.C. &W.E. Powers, 1915), 320-324; *The Sixty-Seventh Ohio Veteran Volunteer Infantry; A Brief Record of Its Four Years of Service in the Civil War 1861-1865* (Massilon, Ohio: Ohio Printing and Publishing Company, 1922), 13-14; Alfred S. Roe, *The Twenty-fourth regiment, Massachusetts volunteers, 1861-1866* (Worcester, Massachusetts: Twenty-Fourth Veteran Association, 1907), 302-303; Johnson Hagood, *Memoirs of the War of Secession* (Columbia, South Carolina: The State Company, 1910), 251-252; Joshua Hilary Hudson, *Sketches and Reminiscences,* (Columbia, South Carolina: The State Company, 1903), 38; John J. Craven, *Prison Life of Jefferson Davis* (New York: Carleton, 1866), 12-17; William Glenn Robertson, *Back Door to Richmond; The Bermuda Hundred Campaign, April--June 1864* (Newark: University of Delaware Press, 1987), 221-222.

56 William T. Sherman, *Memoirs of General William T. Sherman: By Himself, In Two Volumes, Volume II* (New York: D. Appleton and Company, 1891), 59.

57 Joseph C. Carter, ed., *Magnolia Journey; A Union Veteran Revisits the Former Confederate States* (Tuscaloosa, Alabama: The University of Alabama Press, 1974), 22-24.

58 Dennis Hart Mahan, *A Treatise on Field Fortification, Containing Instructions on the Methods of Laying Out, Constructing, Defending, and Attacking Intrenchments* (Richmond, Virginia: West and Johnson, 1862), 1-2, 43-49.

59 National Park Service, *Civil War Defenses of Washington Historic Resources Study* (Washington, DC), Part I, Chapter 5; Part II Chapter 1, accessed February 20, 2022. https://www.nps.gov/parkhistory/online_books/civilwar/hrst.htm W. Springer Menge and J. August Shimrak, eds., *The Civil War Notebook of Daniel Chisolm; A Chronicle of Daily Life in the Union Army* (New York: Ballantine Books, 1989), 18-20.

60 Donald Gordon, ed., M.L. Gordon's experiences in the Civil War: From His Narrative, Letters and Diary (Boston: Privately Printed, 1922), 62-63.

61 James C. Elliott, *The Southern Soldier Boy; A Thousand Shots for the Confederacy* (Raleigh, North Carolina: Edwards and Broughton Printing Company, 1907), 21.

62 Robert J. Forman, et al., *Bermuda Hundred Campaign Tour Guide* (Chesterfield, Virginia: Chesterfield Historical Society, 2010), 38.

63 "A Voice from Henrico," *The Daily State Journal*, Richmond, Virginia, January 21, 1873, 1.

64 John T. Trowbridge, edited by Gordon Carroll, *The Desolate South, 1865-1866; A Picture of the Battlefields and of the Devastated Confederacy* (New York: Duell, Sloan and Pearce, 1956), 76-77.

65 National Park Service, *Civil War Defenses of Washington Historic Resources Study* Part I, Chapter 2.

66 Trowbridge, 70; Carter, 19, 23; Henry Latham, *Black and White: A Journal of Three Months' Tour in the United States* (London: Macmillan and Co., 1867), 106.

67 Theodore Lyman, personal journal, unpublished, transcribed by David Lowe, National Park Service Historian, Washington, DC; Carter, 41; Trowbridge, 51.

68 "Virginia Battle Fields," *Saline County Journal*, August 25, 1881, 1.

69 Anthony Azola, *The Effect of Management on Erosion of Civil War Battlefield Earthworks* (Master's Thesis, Virginia Tech, 2001), 8-12.

70 Carter, 2-3.

71 National Park Service, *Civil War Defenses of Washington Historic Resources Study* Part II, Chapter 3. John T. Willett, *A History of Richmond National Battlefield Park* (National Park Service, Privately Printed, 1957), 37-48.

72 Numerous articles editorials and letters to the editor appeared in local newspapers in the weeks after Via destroyed them. This account has relied primarily on the community newspaper *Herald Progress* (Ashland, Virginia) issues of September 19, 1990, September 26, 1990, and December 12, 1990, as well as Mitch Zemel, "Trench Warfare is Surprising to Hanover County Landowner," *Richmond Times-Dispatch*, September 25, 1990.

73 Robertson, 221-222.

74 Congressional Medal of Honor Society, Engle, James E., accessed February 20, 2022. http://www.cmohs.org/recipient-detail/410/engle-james-e.php

75 Conversation with David Lowe, National Park Service historian, Washington, DC

76 Azola, 47, 54.

77 Drew Gilpin Faust, *This Republic of Suffering; Death and the American Civil War* (New York: Alfred A. Knopf, 2008), 146; Reiko Hillyer, "Relics of Reconciliation: The Confederate Museum and Civil War

Memory in the New South," *The Public Historian* 33, No. 4 (November 2011), 54.

CHAPTER 4

78 Thomas P. Smith, *The Spice Mill on the Marsh* (Norfolk Downs, MA: Pneumatic Scale Corporation, 1925), 7-9; "Slade's Mill Apartments," Slade's Mill Apartments, accessed February 20, 2022. http://www.sladesmill.com.

79 "Ten Existing Northeast Tide Mills," Tide Mill Institute, accessed February 20, 2022. https://www.tidemillinstitute.org/ten-existing-tide-mills/_The Tide Mill Institute is the only organized American body devoted to the study and preservation of tide mills, lists ten original, existing tide mills in the northeastern United States.

80 Smith, 17-20; "The Colonial Slade Mill Starts a Spice Empire in Rever, Mass." New England Historical Society, accessed February 20, 2022. https://www.newenglandhistoricalsociety.com/the-colonial-slade-mill-starts-a-spice-empire-in-revere-mass-ire/.

81 This is a rather simplified version of the fundamental theory of tide mills, although the reality is that sophisticated engineering went into allowing them to capture as much energy as possible. The Tide Mill Institute offers a collection of descriptions of various designs of tide mills. "Definition of a Tide Mill," Tide Mill Institute, accessed February 20, 2022. https://www.tidemillinstitute.org/definition-of-a-tide-mill/.

82 Earle Warren, "The Saltwater Mills of Maine in Context: A Preliminary Exploration, for The Mills Archive." May 2012, 14. Warren is an independent tide mill scholar and longtime leading member of the Tide Mill Institute.

83 Ibid, 12-14.

84 Alice Gertrude Lapham, *The Old Planters of Beverly in Massachusetts & The Thousand Acre Grant* (Carlisle, Massachusetts: Applewood Books, 1930), 54-55.

85 Library of Congress, Prints & Photographs Division, HABS, MA-2-92. https://www.loc.gov/resource/hhh.ma0633.sheet?sp=1&st=gallery, accessed June 1, 2020.

86 National Park Service, National Register of Historic Places Inventory – Nomination Form Available on Virginia Department of Historic Resources website, accessed February 20, 2022. https://www.dhr.virginia.gov/VLR_to_transfer/PDFNoms/057-0008_Poplar_Grove_House&-Mill_1969_DRAFT_Nomination.pdf

87 In 2018 I wrote a feature article for a regional magazine about Poplar Grove, and during the course of reporting, I interviewed the owner as we walked around the mill and estate grounds. Ben Swenson "Treasure

of the Tide," *Distinction*, August 2018, accessed February 20, 2022. https://distinctionva.com/part-4-the-treasure-of-the-tide/

88 "Hydropower Explained; Tidal Power," United States Energy Information Administration, accessed February 20, 2022. https://www.eia.gov/energyexplained/index.php?page=hydropower_tidal

89 "History of Souther Tide Mill," Souther Tide Mill, accessed February 20, 2022. https://southertidemill.org/

90 Stewart Kampel, "The Windmills of Eastern Long Island," *The New York Times*, July 17, 1987. https://www.nytimes.com/1987/07/17/arts/the-windmills-of-eastern-long-island.html.

Michal Kucick. "Interpretation program for the Van Wyck Lefferts Tide Mill; A Thesis in Historic Preservation Presented to the Faculties of the University of Pennsylvania in Partial Fulfillment of the Requirements for the Degree of Master of Science," Master's Thesis (University of Pennsylvania, 1994), 26-28. https://repository.upenn.edu/cgi/viewcontent.cgi?referer=https://www.google.com/&httpsredir=1&article=1280&context=hp_theses

91 "Van Wyck-Lefferts Tide Mill Tour," Huntington Historical Society, accessed February 20, 2022. http://huntingtonhistoricalsociety.org/van-wyck-lefferts-tide-mill/.

92 Kucick, 48. Although some studies of the mill have pegged its origin in 1793, this thesis claims a broader window, only that the mill was there later than 1793 and earlier than 1797.

CHAPTER 5

93 There are several reliable though contradictory firsthand accounts of John Wilkes Booth's capture, and while it's hard to reconcile all these years later two versions of the exact same scene, I've used my best judgment to rely more on those accounts that match the description furnished in separate primary sources, were recorded closer in time to the actual event and seem to be the least influenced by bias. These are the primary sources I have used to reconstruct the events of April 25-26, 1865:

Betsy Fleet and Richard Baynham Garrett, "A Chapter of Unwritten History: Richard Baynham Garrett's Account of the Flight and Death of John Wilkes Booth." The Virginia Magazine of History and Biography, Vol. 71, No. 4 (October 1963), pp. 387-407; "J. Wilkes Booth's Death, The Story of His Capture Told by Capt. E.P. Doherty." No Author. *New York Times,* January 18, 1895, p. 16; Lucinda Holloway, "Capture of Wilkes Booth." Richard Henry Garrett, Letter to the Editor of the *New York Herald;* "Useless! Useless! Some New Facts About the Death of Wilkes Booth" *The Forest Republican* Tionesta, Pennsylvania, February 1, 1882. The correspondent gives a transcription of a conversation with William Garrett; "J. Wilkes Booth's Death, The Story Graphically Told Once More, An Interesting Description of the Pursuit of the Murderer by Lieut. L. B. Baker," Who Had Command of the Party" *New York Times,* December 26, 1879, p. 3; "John Wilkes Booth. New and Interesting Facts Concerning His Pursuit and Death" *Staunton Spectator,* July 7, 1886, p. 1. This is another account by Richard Garrett's sister-in-law Lucinda Holloway, who was present when Booth showed up at Locust Hill; "Only Man Now Living Who Saw Booth Die Tells the Story of His Last Hours" *The Sun,* February 11, 1917, p. 5; "True Story of the Capture of John Wilkes Booth by William Garrett, Lent, VA," Confederate Veteran, Vol. XXIX, number 4, April 1921, p. 129-130.

94 Several well-respected works give graphic and detailed accounts of the moments surrounding Lincoln's shooting. The sources I have consulted are:
Michael W. Kauffman, *American Brutus: John Wilkes Booth and the Lincoln Conspiracies.* New York: Random House, 2004; Edward Steers, Jr., *Blood on the Moon, The Assassination of Abraham Lincoln.* Lexington: University Press of Kentucky, 2001; James L. Swanson, *Manhunt; The 12-Day Chase for Lincoln's Killer.* New York: Harper Perennial, 2006.

95 War Department Proclamation, April 20, 1865.

96 *Manhunt*

97 From the diary taken off John Wilkes Booth after he was shot at the Garrett Farm.

98 1860, 1870 census for Caroline County, Virginia; 1860 slave schedule, U.S. Census, Caroline County, Virginia; Harry Lee Garrett, *Garrett History: History of the Garrett Family of Essex and Caroline Counties of Virginia Beginning with William Garrett, Born 1752, Soldier in the American Revolution, Died July 11, 1825.*, privately published, 1962.

99 1850 agricultural schedule Caroline County, Virginia shows Richard Garrett with 475 improved acres, 244 undeveloped.

100 All the contemporary accounts of Booth's arrival agree on these facts. Richard Baynham Garrett remembers seeing Booth's "J.W.B." tattoo on his forearm in a private letter to A.R. Taylor, Oct 24, 1907; Constance Head, "J.W.B. His Initials in India Ink," *The Virginia Magazine of History and Biography,* July 1982, Vol. 90, no. 3., 359-366; *Manhunt*, 279.

101 *Manhunt*, 279 describes Herold continuing on to Bowling Green. So does the Congressional War Claims Committee Report.

102 There are a number of contemporary photographs of the house which give a good idea of the visual appearance, and the Works Progress Administration Historical Inventory Report titled "Garrett House; Where Booth Died" prepared by Selma Farmer on February 17, 1937, also

gives good descriptions of the interior, exterior and deterioration of the Garrett House.

103 The contemporary accounts cited above all agree on these details.

104 The contemporary accounts disagree somewhat on the exact verbiage used, but all agree on the back-and-forth squabbling and demands of Baker, Conger, and Booth. The exact words written here come from Baker's account in the *New York Times*, December 26, 1879.

105 Swanson, 329, 344; Kauffman, 311; "Lincoln's Avenger and His Sad Fate" by J.E.L., *Washington Post*, April 13, 1913.

106 Baker's account in the *New York Times*, December 26, 1879.

107 Baker, Doherty, Holloway accounts all agree with this.

108 Congressional War Claims Committee Report.

109 1860 and 1870 U.S. Censuses, Caroline County, Virginia; Congressional War Claims Committee Report.

110 *Evening Star*, April 15, 1865, Third Edition, 4 o'clock p.m., "Assassination of the President."

111 Ibid.; "The Arrest of the Supposed Booth," *Liverpool Mercury*, May 8, 1865; Swanson, 257.

112 Holloway's accounts, "Capture of Wilkes Booth" and "John Wilkes Booth. New and Interesting Facts."

113 "Saw Wilkes Booth Die: One of the Soldiers Who Assisted in the Assassin's Capture," *Washington Post*, December 28, 1890, p. 16.

114 Holloway's account "John Wilkes Booth. New and Interesting Facts."

115 "Attention, Visitors! G.A.R. Members and Others." Advertisement. *The Times* [Washington, DC], October 5, 1902, p. 14, cols. 2-3.

116 Swanson, 276, 373-374. *Evening Bulletin* [Maysville, KY], April 10, 1890, "A Historic Place Sold."

117 Holloway's accounts, "Capture of Wilkes Booth" and "John Wilkes Booth. New and Interesting Facts."

118 "True Story of the Capture of John Wilkes Booth by William Garrett, Lent, VA."

119 Richard B. Garrett to J. B. Bentley, personal letter, February 7th, 1882, held by the Virginia Historical Society.

120 Farmer, Historical Inventory Report, p. 4.

121 History of Fort A.P. Hill, *Wealthy in Heart*, Frank Wilder, "Booth's End Now 'Marked' by Brambles," *Washington Post*, April 22, 1951, p. B8.

122 Personal communication with the Virginia Department of Transportation.

CHAPTER 6

123 William T. Donnelly, "Wooden Ships and the Submarine Menace," *International Marine Engineering* 22, no. 6 (June 1917): 251; "Torpe-

doed U.S. Schooner Carried No Contraband," *The Day Book*, February 15, 1917, LAST EDITION; "The Suppression of the U-Boat Menace the Supreme Duty of the Hour," *The Sun*, May 04, 1917.

124 John P. Adams "Six Ways to Build Wooden Ships," *Yankee*, November 1970, 102-109, 219; Hough, 272.

125 The number of wooden steamships that officials with the United States Shipping Board and President Woodrow Wilson's cabinet envisioned was 1,000, but the total number that the government contracted was 731. Louis A. Hough, *A Fleet to be Forgotten; The Wooden Freighters of World War I* (San Francisco: San Francisco Maritime History Press, 2009), 16; Donald G. Shomette, *Ghost Fleet of Mallows Bay and Other Tales of the Lost Chesapeake* (Centreville, Maryland: Tidewater Publishers, 1996), 230; George J. Baldwin, "Solving the Problem of the Ships," *International Marine Engineering*, 22, no. 6 (June 1917): 248.

126 William J. Williams, *The Wilson Administration and the Shipbuilding Crisis of 1917; Steel Ships and Wooden Steamers* (New York: The Edwin Mellen Press, 199), 64-65; Hough, 17.

127 Adams, "Six Ways to Build Wooden Ships," 104-106; Hough, 263.

128 "Six Ways to Build Wooden Ships," 104; Hough, 145, 290.

129 William Joe Webb, "The United States Wooden Steamship Program During World War I," *The American Neptune* 35, no. 4 (October 1975): 283. Hough, 211.

130 James L. Bonnett, "Wooden Ships and Their Iron Men," *Sunday Sun Magazine*, November 20, 1960, 2.

131 "Government to Sell Ferris-Type Wood Hulls," *The Nautical Gazette*, November 8, 1919.

132 Robert H. Burgess, *This Was Chesapeake Bay*, (Cambridge, Maryland: Cornell Maritime Press, 1963), 168; Shomette, 232.

133 Shomette, 233; Webb, 286-287.

134 Shomette, 237, 247.

135 Shomette, 244-247, 255-258.

136 "Opinion Issued on Hulls of 169 Sunken Craft," *Washington Post*, May 5, 1935.

137 Frederick Tilp, *This Was Potomac River*, (Bladensburg, Maryland: Self-published, 1978), 88.

138 Robert Fountain Hedges Sea Scout Log as recorded in Tilp, 265; Shomette, 260-261; "Opinion Issued on Hulls of 169 Sunken Craft," *Washington Post*, May 5, 1935; Tilp, 294.

139 Shomette, 271-275.

140 "Sickles Acts to Rid River of Derelicts." *Washington Post*, September 9, 1964.

141 Karen Hyneckeal, "Old Ships Controversy Renewed," *The Baltimore Sun*, February 10, 1967.

142 "A Dangerous and Dirty Ghost Fleet," *Washington Post,* no date, found in Mallows Bay file, Mariners' Museum Library, Newport News, Virginia; Shomette, 283-284; Quoted from U.S. Congress, House of Representatives, Report No. 91-1761, "Protecting America's Estuaries: The Potomac," 91st Congress, 2nd Session, 1970, 7-8.
143 Robert Fountain Hedges Sea Scout Log as recorded in Tilp, 265.
144 Pelton, Tom, "Habitat for Hope," *Save the Bay* 37, No. 3, Fall 2011, 30; U.S. Congress, House of Representatives, Report No. 91-1761, 7-8.
145 Hardenberg's life has been reconstructed from the following contemporary newspaper accounts: "'Lonesome Charlie' Quits Desert Island; Ten Year a Hermit," *The Washington Times,* September 26, 1920, 1-2; "Hermit, Ten Years on Island, Comes Back to Civilization," *New York Tribune,* September 27, 1920, 1; "Became Island Hermit 10 Years on Wager," *Peninsula Enterprise,* October 9, 1920; "Modern Crusoe on Small Island," *The Tuscaloosa News,* August 15, 1930, 4; "Lonely Hermit Has Spent 22 Years on Small Bay Island," *Eastern Shore News,* August 15, 1930; "Watts Island Hermit Pays Call Thursday," *Eastern Shore News,* October 10, 1930; "It's Mr. and Mrs. Over on Little Watts Island Now," *Eastern Shore News,* August 23, 1931; "Hermit for 23 Years Takes Bride At Last," *Washington Post,* September 1, 1931, 12; "Hardenbergs Not Content to Leave Things As Are Now," *Eastern Shore News,* September 4, 1931; "No More Solitaire for Island Hermit," *Plattsburgh Daily Press,* September 23, 1931, 8; "Island Hermit Through With Solitaire; Tardy Romance Leads Him to Altar," *The Palm Beach Post,* October 14, 1931, 3; "Homing Pigeon Stops to Visit the Hardenburgs," *Eastern Shore News,* September 16, 1932; "Former Hermit, Little Watts, Embarks on Last Journey, *Eastern Shore News,* March 5, 1937; Editorial, *Peninsula Enterprise,* November 29, 1962, 4; "50 Years Ago," *Eastern Shore News,* August 27, 1987. See also Kirk Mariner, "The Hermit of Watts Island," *Chesapeake Bay Magazine,* February 1983, 28-30.
146 William W. Warner, *Beautiful Swimmers; Watermen, Crabs and the Chesapeake Bay* (New York: Penguin Books, 1977), 5. John R. Wennersten, *The Chesapeake: An Environmental Biography* (Baltimore, Maryland: Maryland Historical Society, 2001), 3-5. Richard Dent, Jr., *Chesapeake Prehistory; Old Traditions, New Directions* (New York: Plenum Press, 1995), 69-85.
147 Helen C. Rountree, Wayne E. Clark, and Kent Mountford, *John Smith's Chesapeake Voyages, 1607-1609* (Charlottesville, Virginia: University of Virginia Press, 2007), 31.
148 Cultural Resources, Inc., "An Assessment of Cultural Resource Potential Within "Uppards" and Goose Island, Tangier Island, Accomack County, Virginia," Virginia Department of Historic Resources, File Number 2003-1046, Richmond, Virginia, September 2003, 11-12; Helen C.

Rountree and Thomas E. Davidson, *Eastern Shore Indians of Virginia and Maryland* (Charlottesville, Virginia: University of Virginia Press, 1997), 34-38.

149 William B. Cronin, *Disappearing Islands of the Chesapeake* (Baltimore, Maryland: The Johns Hopkins University Press, 2005), 4.

150 "Cream of Current Events," *The Lancaster Intelligencer,* April 17, 1890, 1; "Talk of the Day," *New-York Tribune,* July 28, 1899, 6.

151 *Peninsula Enterprise*, June 7, 1884 (Untitled, beginning "Mr. S. A. Byrd, with N. W. Nock and family returned Saturday afternoon from a very pleasant excursion down the bay..."); "'Lonesome Charlie' Quits Desert Island; Ten Year a Hermit," *The Washington Times*, September 26, 1920, 1-2.

152 "Modern Crusoe on Small Island," *The Tuscaloosa News,* August 15, 1930, 4.

153 "'Lonesome Charlie' Quits Desert Island; Ten Year a Hermit," *The Washington Times,* September 26, 1920, 1-2; "Modern Crusoe on Small Island," *The Tuscaloosa News,* August 15, 1930, 4; "World War I Draft Registration Cards, 1917-1918," digital images, Ancestry.com accessed February 20, 2022. Charles Hardenberg, serial no. 285, order no. 2947, County of Accomack Draft Board Precinct, citing World War I Selective Service Draft Registration Cards, NARA microfilm publications M1509, no specific roll cited.

154 "Modern Crusoe on Small Island," *The Tuscaloosa News,* August 15, 1930, 4; "Lonely Hermit Has Spent 22 Years on Small Bay Island," *Eastern Shore News,* August 15, 1930.

155 "Lonely Hermit Has Spent 22 Years on Small Bay Island," *Eastern Shore News,* August 15, 1930; "Island Hermit Through with Solitaire; Tardy Romance Leads Him to Altar," *The Palm Beach Post,* October 14, 1931, 3.

156 "'Lonesome Charlie' Quits Desert Island; Ten Year a Hermit," *The Washington Times,* September 26, 1920, 1-2; "Modern Crusoe on Small Island," *The Tuscaloosa News,* August 15, 1930, 4.

157 Mariner, "The Hermit of Watts Island," 30.

158 "'Lonesome Charlie' Quits Desert Island; Ten Year a Hermit," *The Washington Times*, September 26, 1920, 1-2.

159 Donald G. Shomette, *Pirates on the Chesapeake: Being a True History of Pirates, Picaroons, and Raiders on the Chesapeake Bay, 1610-1807* (Centreville, Maryland: Tidewater Publishers, 1985), 70-72. John R. Wennersten, *The Oyster Wars of the Chesapeake Bay* Centreville, Maryland: Tidewater Publishers, 1981), 61-62. Cronin, 143-144.

160 "Raising Black Cats," *The Galveston Daily News,* January 11, 1892, 7; Cronin, 58; Kent Mountford, "Most of what now exists of eroding James Island is memories," *Bay Journal*, September 1, 2003.

161 "Modern Crusoe on Small Island," *The Tuscaloosa News,* August 15, 1930, 4.

162 "Watts Island Hermit Pays Call Thursday," *Eastern Shore News*, October 10, 1930; Mariner, "The Hermit of Watts Island," 29. Ralph T. Whitelaw, *Virginia's Eastern Shore; A History of Northampton and Accomack Counties, Volume Two* (Gloucester, Massachusetts: Peter Smith, 1968), 973-974.

163 "It's Mr. and Mrs. Over on Little Watts Island Now," *Eastern Shore News,* August 23, 1931; "Hermit for 23 Years Takes Bride At Last," *Washington Post,* September 1, 1931, 12; "Hardenbergs Not Content to Leave Things As Are Now," *Eastern Shore News,* September 4, 1931; "No More Solitaire for Island Hermit," *Plattsburgh Daily Press*, September 23, 1931, 8; "Island Hermit Through With Solitaire; Tardy Romance Leads Him to Altar," *The Palm Beach Post*, October 14, 1931, 3; See also the marriage registration for Charles Hardenberg and Katherine Seipel, August 1931, Accomack County.

164 "'Lonesome Charlie' Quits Desert Island; Ten Year a Hermit," *The Washington Times*, September 26, 1920, 1-2.

165 "Modern Crusoe on Small Island," *The Tuscaloosa News,* August 15, 1930, 4.

166 Rountree, Clarke, and Mountford, 83-85; National Park Service, John Smith's Shallop, accessed February 20, 2022. https://www.nps.gov/articles/000/john-smith-shallop.htm; Captain John Smith, *The Generall Historie of Virginia, New England & the Summer Isles,* (Glasgow: James MacLehose and Sons, 1907)

167 Diane Tennant, "A Little Storm," A ten-part series, *The Virginian-Pilot,* September 18-27, 2011; Mariner, "The Hermit of Watts Island," 30.

168 Mariner, "The Hermit of Watts Island," 30. The 1940 United States Census for Accomack County, Virginia, Metompkin Magisterial District, Accomack County Alms House.

169 Interview with J. Court Stephenson, along with his presentation "March 24, 2010," PowerPoint file, 57; Wennersten, *The Oyster Wars of the Chesapeake Bay.*

170 Mariner, "The Hermit of Watts Island," 30; Cronin, 103-106; Robert Burgess, *This was Chesapeake Bay* (Cambridge, Maryland: Cornell Maritime Press, 1963), 200-201.

171 Interview with J. Court Stephenson; Cronin, 164-175.

CHAPTER 8

172 Amy Randolph, "Overview of the Laurel Run Mine Fire; Borough of Laurel Run, Luzerne County, Pennsylvania," Pennsylvania Depart-

ment of Conservation and Natural Resources, August 2002. Randolph prepared this departmental publication for an internship field trip in 2002, and it is one of the few professional assessments of the history and scope of the Laurel Run mine fire; Henry A. Dierks, R. H. Whaite and A. H. Harvey, "Three Mine Fire Control Projects in Northeastern Pennsylvania," U.S. Department of the Interior, Bureau of Mines, Information Circular 8524, 5.

173 Barbara Freese, *Coal; A Human History* (New York: Penguin Books, 2003), 111-112.

174 David DeKok, *Fire Underground; The Ongoing Tragedy of the Centralia Mine Fire* (Guilford, Conn., Glove Pequot Press, 2010), 19 – 26; Joan Quigley, *The Day the Earth Caved In; An American Mining Tragedy* (New York: Random House Trade Paperbacks, 2009), 7-8. These two works provide the most comprehensive account of the Centralia mine fire and its long aftermath. While the facts surrounding the case are nearly identical in both accounts, the authors disagree on the initial cause of the fire. DeKok claims that the fire was intentionally set to clear debris from the landfill. Quigley says that hot cinders in refuse dumped in the landfill started the blaze.

175 Quigley, prologue, xiii-xvi. DeKok, 137-138.

176 DeKok, 237–239 (also the chapter "Victory"). Quigley, 131-135, 150-164.

177 DeKok, 240-245 ("Victory") and Quigley, 213 - 214.

178 Quigley, 29-48.

179 Kevin Krajik, "Fire in the Hole," *Smithsonian Magazine*, May 2005, accessed February 20. 2022, https://www.smithsonianmag.com/science-nature/fire-in-the-hole-77895126/ Miss Cellania, "5 Places That Are Still on Fire," *Mental Floss*, September 24, 2013. http://mentalfloss.com/article/52869/5-places-are-still-fire.

180 John Grammer, Jr., "An Account of the Coal Mines in the vicinity of Richmond, Virginia, communicated to the editor in a letter from Mr. John Grammer, Jr.," *The American Journal of Science*, vol 1., 1819, 125-130.

181 Mary Kelley. *Images of America; Coal in Campbell County* (Charleston, S.C.: Arcadia Publishing, 2013), 21-28.

182 Kristin Ohlson, "Earth on Fire," *Discover Magazine*. July-August 2010.

183 Kathleen Purcell Munley, *The West Side Carbondale, Pennsylvania Mine Fire* (Scranton, PA: University of Scranton Press, 2013.

184 Interview with Joe Gregory

185 Randolph, 2; Dierks, 9-14.

186 Personal correspondence with Patricia Hester, April 2015.

187 Randolph, 2-3. Dierks, 9-15.

188 Randolph, 5. Dierks, 15.

189 Personal correspondence with Tim Altares, geologist at Pennsylvania Department of Environmental Protection, 2015.

CHAPTER 9

190 Although he was relentless in his pursuit of business affairs, obituaries written upon his death on December 8, 1885, praised him effusively for his conspicuous consumption, as well as his contributions to equestrianism, science, and art. See "William H. Vanderbilt," *New York Times* (New York, NY), December 9, 1885, and "W.H. Vanderbilt Dead," *New-York Tribune* (New York, NY), December 9, 1885.

191 Grouseland Tours' website: https://www.grouseland.com. Southern Alleghenies Conservancy, "Pike 2 Bike: Southern Alleghenies Conservancy Trail Network Master Plan and Adaptive Re-use Study" (Pannsylvania, Gannett Fleming, May 2006), 3. Hereafter cited as "SAC Master Plan."

192 Herbert Harwood Jr., *The Railroad That Never Was: Vanderbilt, Morgan and the South Pennsylvania Railroad* (Bloomington: Indiana University Press, 2010), 19-20. Lorret Treese, *Railroads of Pennsylvania: Fragments of the Past in the Keystone Landscape* (Mechanicsburg, PA: Stackpole Books, 2003), 189-190. Albro Martin, "Crisis of Rugged Individualism: The West Shore. South Pennsylvania Railroad Affair, 1880-1885." *The Pennsylvania Magazine of History and Biography* 93, no. 2 (1969), 221-222.

193 Harwood, 23, 25, 66, 69-71. Schrotenboer took me to one of the abandoned culverts made by Italian stonemasons, and it was nearly a work of art, a neat and sturdy tunnel with arching stone, made of locally quarried stone. Though covered with the detritus of a mature forest, it has survived with very little weathering.

194 Harwood, 81-84. Martin, 234. The "Vanderbilt's Folly" reference: Nick Malawskey, "Tunnel Vision," Penn Live, accessed February 20, 2022. https://www.pennlive.com/projects/2015/pa-turnpike-tunnels/.

195 Pauline Shieh and Kim Parry, "The Building of the Great Pennsylvania Turnpike," a webpage on The Literary & Cultural Heritage Map of Pennsylvania, Pennsylvania Center for the Book, Penn State University, accessed February 20, 2022. https://pabook.libraries.psu.edu/literary-cultural-heritage-map-pa/feature-articles/building-great-pennsylvania-turnpike. Mitchell Dakelman and Neal Schorr. *The Pennsylvania Turnpike*. Images of America. (Mount Pleasant, SC: Arcadia Publishing, 2004), 29. "The Superhighway." In *Pennsylvania Cavalcade*, edited by Pennsylvania Writers' Project Work Projects Administration, 408-21. Philadelphia: University of Pennsylvania Press, 1942.

196 Dakelman and Schorr, 21. "Turnpike History" on the official website of the Pennsylvania Turnpike, accessed February 20, 2022. https://www.paturnpike.com/yourTurnpike/ptc_history.aspx.
197 "The Superhighway," 416. "Turnpike History," Shieh and Parry.
198 "The Superhighway," 410.
199 Shieh and Parry. "Turnpike History."
200 Kelly Kissel. "50-Year-Old Pennsylvania Turnpike Provided Modern Road to the Future," *Los Angeles Times*, October 7, 1990. "The Superhighway," 409. "Turnpike History."
201 Sammarco, Anthony Mitchell. *A History of Howard Johnson's; How a Massachusetts Soda Fountain Became an American Icon.* (Charleston, SC: The History Press, 2013), Chapter 4.
202 Schrotenboer has among his collection of Pennsylvania Turnpike memorabilia an original HoJo menu.
203 According to the Turnpike's official history, planners thought that 1.4 million automobiles would use the road annually, but early on it became clear that the figure was about 2.3 million. See "Turnpike History."
204 Malawsky, Nick. "The Toll," *Central PA Magazine*, July/August 2015, 35-39. Webster, Larry. "The Secret Racing Test Tunnel No One Wants to Talk About," *Road & Track*, January 9, 2015.
205 Early turnpike landscapers intentionally planted flowering and fruit trees for their aesthetic value to the motorists on the roadway, according to "The Superhighway," 409.
206 Bats took up residence in the abandoned South Penn Railroad tunnels long before they became part of the Pennsylvania Turnpike. In the late 1930s, scientist Charles Mohr observed large colonies of bats residing in the abandoned passages. Mohr, Charles E. "Bat Tagging in Pennsylvania Turnpike Tunnels." *Journal of Mammalogy* 23, no. 4 (1942): 375-79.
207 "Master Plan," 3-4.
208 Joe Penhall. *The Road.* DVD. Directed by John Hillcoat. Dallas, TX: 2929 Productions, 2009.

CHAPTER 10

209 "Bridge Day," New River Gorge Bridge Day Commission, accessed February 20, 2022. https://officialbridgeday.com/.
210 National Register of Historic Places, New River Gorge Bridge, Fayetteville, WV, National Register # 13000603; "Autumn Colors Express," Rail Excursion Management Co., accessed February 20, 2022. https://www.autumncolorexpresswv.com/.
211 National Register of Historic Places, Kay Moor; Kay Moor No. 1 Coal Mine, Fayetteville, WV, National Register # 90001641; "Kaymoor,"

New River Gorge National River, National Park Service, accessed February 20, 2022. https://www.nps.gov/neri/learn/historyculture/kaymoor.htm.

212 National Register of Historic Places, Kay Moor.

213 National Register of Historic Places, Kay Moor.

214 "Geology of the New River Gorge," New River Gorge National River, National Park Service, accessed February 20, 2022. https://www.nps.gov/neri/learn/nature/geology.htm; Noah Adams, *Far Appalachia; Following the New River North* (New York: Dell Publishing, 2001); "West Virginia Earth Science Studies: Geology of the New River Gorge," West Virginia Geological & Economic Survey, accessed February 20, 2022. http://www.wvgs.wvnet.edu/www/geology/geoles01.htm.

215 "New River Gorge, West Virginia," NASA Earth Observatory, accessed February 20, 2022. https://earthobservatory.nasa.gov/images/5019/new-river-gorge-west-virginia.

216 "West Virginia Earth Science Studies: Beneath the New River Gorge," West Virginia Geological & Economic Survey, accessed February 20, 2022. http://www.wvgs.wvnet.edu/www/geology/geoles02.htm

217 U.S. Energy Information Administration, "Annual Coal Report 2018," Washington, DC: U.S. Department of Energy, October 2021, accessed February 20, 2022, https://www.eia.gov/coal/annual/; Ronald L. Lewis, "The Darkest Abode of Man," *The Virginia Magazine of History and Biography*, vol. 87, no. 2 (April 1979), 190-202. Thomas Jefferson, *Notes on the State of Virginia*. (London: Printed for John Stockdale, 1787), published online by The Federalist Papers Project, https://www.thefederalistpapers.org/wp-content/uploads/2012/12/Thomas-Jefferson-Notes-On-The-State-Of-Virginia.pdf.

218 John Florin. "Appalachia." *The New Encyclopedia of Southern Culture: Volume 2: Geography*, edited by Richard Pillsbury, by Charles Reagan Wilson, University of North Carolina Press, 2006, 42–45.

219 Melody Bragg, *Window to the Past*. Beaver, West Virginia: GEM Publications, 2011. 32-33.

220 Bragg, 31.

221 Fortunately, the New River Gorge's coal boom is well documented in pictures. See Bragg, 35-37. Also see Stan Cohen, *King Coal: A Pictorial Heritage of West Virginia Coal Mining*. Charleston, WV: Quarrier Press, 1984. The chapter entitled "Coke" 45 – 54 and "Company Stores and Towns" 55 – 80 both offer numerous pictures of coke ovens and towns. See also J. Scott Legg and the Fayette County Chamber of Commerce, Images of America: New River Gorge. Mount Pleasant, S.C.: Arcadia Publishing, 2010. Armstrong, Donald, and Charles Yuill. "The Abandoned Mines of the New River Gorge: Health and Safety Hazards and Important Cultural Resources." *Parkways, Gre-*

enways, Riverways: The Way More Beautiful, edited by Woodward S. Bousquet et al., Appalachian State University, Boone, North Carolina, 1989, 261.

222 Cohen 11-14.

223 Bragg, 208 – 211. Good, Gregory and Lynn Stasick. *New River Gorge National River; Administrative History*. Washington, DC: U.S. Department of the Interior, 2008. 22–23.

224 Bragg, 228 – 233, 242-248.

225 Bragg, 16-17.

226 Tiana Hall. "The Homefront and How West Virginians Contributed to World War I" in *Together We Won the Great War; West Virginia and World War I, A West Virginia Archives and History Online Exhibit.* West Virginia Department of Arts, Culture and History, accessed February 20, 2022. https://archive.wvculture.org/history/exhibitsonline/worldwar1/wwoneintroductiontoc.html. See also National Register of Historic Places: Kay Moor.

227 Janet L Fryer. 2010. Ailanthus altissima. In: Fire Effects Information System. U.S. Department of Agriculture, Forest Service, Rocky Mountain Research Station, Fire Sciences Laboratory. https://www.fs.fed.us/database/feis/plants/tree/ailalt/all.html.

228 *New York Times*, May 26, 1950.

229 Fryer, Ailanthus altissima.

230 David R Jackson. "Invasive Weeds Fact Sheet, Tree-of-Heaven (Ailanthus altissima)," The Pennsylvania State University, 2018.

231 National Register of Historic Places, Kay Moor.

232 Ibid.

CHAPTER 11

233 Charles Mitchell, "A Monstrous Tow . . . and The Concrete Ship S.S. Willis Slater," *The Master Mate & Pilot*, April 1987.

234 "Concrete Ships Help Carry War Supplies," *Washington Post,* June 11, 1944.

235 Frederic C. Lane, Ships for Victory; *A History of Shipbuilding Under the U.S. Maritime Commission in World War II*, (Baltimore: The Johns Hopkins Press, 1951), 628-629.

236 *Concrete Ships, A Possible Solution of the Shipping Problem,* Chicago: Portland Cement Association, December 1917; "Reinforced Concrete Shipbuilding--A Field for Pioneers," International Marine Engineering, July 1917, 1; "Faith in Concrete Ships," New York Times, March 17, 1918; William J. Williams, "The American Concrete Shipbuilding Program of World War I," *The American Neptune; A Quarterly Journal of Maritime History* 52, no. 1 (Winter 1992): 6, 15.

237 "Concrete Ships: Big Advances Made Since '17 Since First Was

Laid Down," *New York Times*, July 12, 1942; Lane, 628-630; Jean Haviland, "American Concrete Steamers of the First and Second World Wars," *The American Neptune; A Quarterly Journal of Maritime History* 22 (July 1962): 173-175.

238 "Three Concrete Ships Launched," *New York Times*, March 22, 1944; "Arthur N. Talbot, Noted Engineer; Professor Emeritus at Illinois University, Pioneer Designer of Reinforced Concrete, Dies," *New York Times*, April 1, 1932, 13.

239 Haviland, "American Concrete Steamers of the First and Second World Wars," 175; John A. Campbell, *Hulks; The Breakwater Ships of Powell River*, (Powell River, Canada: Works Publishing, 2003), 61.

240 Campbell, 58, 61; Haviland, "American Concrete Steamers of the First and Second World Wars," 181.

241 Mitchell, "A Monstrous Tow."

242 Mitchell, "A Monstrous Tow."

243 Mitchell, "A Monstrous Tow."

244 Haviland, "American Concrete Steamers of the First and Second World Wars," 176-177.

245 Haviland, "American Concrete Steamers of the First and Second World Wars," 177-180.

246 "Audit of Federal Maritime Board and Maritime Administration, Department of Commerce, and the Predecessor Agency, United States Maritime Commission," (Washington, DC: United States Government Printing Office, 1951), 61.

247 "Family Project: 42' Cement Ketch," *National Fisherman*, January 1970.

248 "Removing Ferry Bottlenecks," *New York Times*, March 21, 1948; Mark Di Vincenzo, "Beachgoers Can Thank U.S. Army," *Daily Press*, May 25, 1992.

249 Di Vincenzo, "Beachgoers Can Thank U.S. Army."

250 Campbell, 7-8; "Breakwater of Ships," *Powell River Digester*, Vol. 24 No. 2, March/April 1948, 14-15.

251 Photos MS 342.19.56.01 and MS 342.19.56.02 from folder 56 of the Haviland Collection at the Mariner's Museum in Newport News, VA shows the ships shortly after ferry officials sunk them in late 1948 or early 1949 and by all appearances they are fully rigged. This was corroborated by separate conversations with two Eastern Shore residents, Bill Parr and Ted Boelt, both of whom remember the ships fully rigged and stocked in their earliest days at Kiptopeke.

252 Conversations with Bill Parr and Ted Boelt.

253 This is best illustrated by comparing photographs from the Haviland collection at the Mariner's Museum. Photos MS 342.19.56.01 and 342.19.56.02 show the ships shortly after they arrived. Another pho-

to, MS 342.19.56.03 shows them about seven years later on June 24, 1956. The ships have deteriorated, lost most of their lines and rigging and there is visible deterioration of the hulls.

254 Conversation with local historian Bill Parr.

255 "Ferry Terminal Dedicated Kiptopeke Beach Saturday," *The Northampton Times,* May 4, 1950, 1.

CHAPTER 12

256 Thomas B. Cochran, William M. Arkin, and Milton M. Hoenig, U.S. Nuclear Forces and Capabilities, Nuclear Weapons Databook (Cambridge, Massachusetts: Ballinger Publishing Company, 1984), 45. This source claims that a single Hercules missile could be equipped with a warhead of two, twenty or forty kilotons. Mega-trains of 3.5 miles in length have begun hauling freight in the United States, and have a carrying capacity of 15,500 tons, less than the equivalent amount of explosive power (20,000 pounds of TNT) in a twenty-kiloton warhead. See Stephen Joiner, "Is Bigger Better? 'Monster' Trains vs. Freight Trains," *Popular Mechanics,* February 11, 2010. https://www.popularmechanics.com/technology/infrastructure/a5314/4345689/.

257 *Department of the Army Field Manual FM 44-1; U.S. Army Air Defense Employment.* (Washington, DC: Department of the Army, 1962, Chapter 4, "Air Defense Employment Principles," 17-22, accessed February 20, 2022, http://www.bits.de/NRANEU/others/amd-us-archive/FM44-1(62).pdf; John Derose, "When Nike Meant Missiles: Exploring Local Vestiges of the Cold War," *OAH Magazine of History* 24, no. 4 (2010): 30-34; Christopher John Bright. «Nike Defends Washington: Antiaircraft Missiles in Fairfax County, Virginia, during the Cold War, 1954-1974,» *The Virginia Magazine of History and Biography* 105, no. 3 (1997): 323-327.

258 John Knute Smoley, "Seizing Victory from the Jaws of Deterrence: Preservation and Public Memory of America's Nike Air Defense Missile System," (Doctoral Diss., University of California Santa Barbara and California State University, 2008), 388-396.

259 Timothy W. Layton and H. Eliot Foulds. "Cultural Landscape Report for the Sandy Hook Coastal Defense Batteries, Gateway National Recreation Area," (Boston, MA: Olmsted Center for Landscape Preservation, 2010), 10-11, 124-125, 133.https://www.nps.gov/gate/learn/historyculture/upload/culturallandscap00layt-1.pdf.

260 Ibid., 128-130, 198-201.

261 The Fort Hancock Nike Association has a website, https://ny56nike.weebly.com/. The San Francisco-area Nike site is located at Golden Gate National Recreation Area, https://www.nps.gov/goga/nike-missile-site.htm. Anchorage's Nike battery is on the eastern edge of Fort

Richardson and stewarded by Friends of Nike Site Summit, https://www.nikesitesummit.net. Florida's lone preserved Nike site is in the boundaries of Everglades National Park, https://www.nps.gov/ever/learn/historyculture/hm69.htm.

262 Smoley, 41. Layton, 195-197. Bright, 324 offers a photograph showing an aerial view of a Nike radar site in Lorton, Virginia, similar to what the Fort Hancock building would have looked like.

263 John C. Lonnquest and David F. Winkler. *To Defend and Deter: The Legacy of the United States Cold War Missile Program.* Rock Island, Il: Defense Publishing Service, 1996, 172-173.

264 Layton, 147 offers a good diagram of each of the buildings of the IFC area and their uses.

265 Lonnquest, 177.

266 Layton, 195-197.

267 Lonnquest 173-176 and 182 describes how the launch areas were originally designed for Nike Ajax missiles but then modified to accommodate the larger Hercules. Each magazine could initially hold 12 Ajax missiles but only 8 Hercules missiles after retrofitting.

268 Smoley, 99-100.

269 Smoley 179-187.

270 Bright, 331 and 341, identifies that when Nike sites held the conventional Ajax weapons, open houses for members of the community were a regular feature at the Nike site at Lorton, Virginia, because of the proximity to the nation's capital. The site was a showplace for visiting foreign dignitaries as well. See Smoley, 374, for claim on largest peacetime deployment of military materiel.

271 Smoley, 110.

272 Smoley, 307 shows a picture of C-47, a Nike launch area near Chicago, filled with water. Personal observations by both sight and sound at Nike launch areas around the Chesapeake confirm the presence of water in the launch area's subterranean chambers.

273 The name for the Generator and Frequency Changing and Warhead buildings comes from Layton, 147 and 198.

274 "Gateway National Recreation Area," National Park Service, accessed February 20, 2022. http://www.nps.gov/gateway.

275 The company discontinued these models decades ago, but willing purchasers can still find original, unconstructed models of both the Ajax and Hercules missiles on eBay.

276 "List of Nike missile sites," Wikipedia, accessed February 20, 2022. https://en.wikipedia.org/wiki/List_of_Nike_missile_sites.

277 Smoley, 356.

278 Town of Wayland, Massachusetts, "Wayland Massachusetts Nike Missile Site Stewardship Report." (Wayland, MA, 2016).

About the Author

Ben Swenson is a writer and educator in Williamsburg, Va. A lifelong Virginian, Ben was steeped in the rich history of Tidewater from a young age – an upbringing that exposed him to the region's rich remnants of the past. Ben has written professionally for newspapers and magazines for over two decades, covering a wide range of stories from politics to skydiving. Time and again, these assignments geared Ben toward disappearing history, and not too long into his writing career, Ben realized he had uncovered enough abandoned history to fill a book.

www.ingramcontent.com/pod-product-compliance
Lightning Source LLC
LaVergne TN
LVHW091758230625
814486LV00002B/11

* 9 7 8 1 9 6 2 4 1 6 9 0 0 *